'*Towards Better Disagreement: Relig*
is a thoughtful and compassionate
between those who find some spir......
existence and those that do not. It is marked by a gentle courtesy
towards disputants, without at all ignoring or belittling genuine
disagreements. What makes it remarkably valuable, both for the
more general reader as well as the student, is the wide range
of issues covered from questions about the founders of religion
(like Jesus) to contemporary problems of much concern including
sex and gender, and the nature and place of animals. Highly
recommended.'

*– Michael Ruse, Lucyle T Werkmeister Professor of Philosophy
at Florida State University and author of* Darwinism as
Religion: What Literature Tells Us about Evolution

'This is a terrific little book! I don't know how you managed
to cover so many key issues so clearly and in such a short
space. You have done a remarkably good job: the writing is
clear and accessible; to my mind your tone is perfect because
you emphasize that you want to engage with people, but that,
like them, you do have opinions; this is one of the few times
I really liked boxes because they provided short, pertinent
examples instead of interrupting the text. I would use this text,
in fact I would like to use this text for a class I am giving in
the spring, so I wish it were already published! I very much
liked your introductory discussion about faith vs. reason. That
is such an important issue, and you covered it beautifully with
excellent examples and thought experiments... This was a most
enjoyable read.'

*– Dr. Allison P. Coudert, Paul and Marie Castelfranco
Chair in the Study of Religion University of California*

of related interest

The Forgiveness Project
Stories for a Vengeful Age
Marina Cantacuzino
Forewords by Archbishop Emeritus Desmond Tutu and Alexander McCall Smith
ISBN 978 1 84905 566 6 (Hardback)
ISBN 978 1 78592 000 4 (Paperback)
eISBN 978 1 78450 006 1

Sceptical Christianity
Exploring Credible Belief
Robert Reiss
ISBN 978 1 78592 062 2
eISBN 978 1 78450 318 5

Re-enchanting the Activist
Spirituality and Social Change
Keith Hebden
ISBN 978 1 78592 041 7
eISBN 978 1 78450 295 9

Towards Better Disagreement

Religion and Atheism in Dialogue

PAUL HEDGES

Jessica Kingsley *Publishers*
London and Philadelphia

First published in 2017
by Jessica Kingsley Publishers
73 Collier Street
London N1 9BE, UK
and
400 Market Street, Suite 400
Philadelphia, PA 19106, USA

www.jkp.com

Library of Congress Cataloging in Publication Data
Names: Hedges, Paul (Paul Michael), 1970- author.
Title: Towards better disagreement : religion and atheism in dialogue / Paul
    Hedges.
Description: Philadelphia : Jessica Kingsley Publishers, 2016. | Includes
    index.
Identifiers: LCCN 2016010285 | ISBN 9781785920578 (alk. paper)
Subjects: LCSH: Religions. | Atheism.
Classification: LCC BL80.3 .H435 2016 | DDC 201/.51--dc23 LC record available at
    https://urldefense.proofpoint.com/v2/url?u=https-3A__lccn.loc.gov_2016010285&d
    =BQIFAg&c=euGZstcaTDllvimEN8b7jXrwqOf-v5A_CdpgnVfiiMM&r=jDhEGalRBce
    h95Jy341lNgmWR9tnCifzbrA2NWHfaH8&m=Xdldi1sOYKEVeMA1yP4za-J_
    dpyLAKdqgOJM2nm2hWQ&s=Xy_9BAmcUgNhIyo30YIL_
    jbMVyHqmTYOETooSorVHk8&e=

British Library Cataloguing in Publication Data
A CIP catalogue record for this book is available from the British Library.
ISBN 978 1 78592 057 8
eISBN 978 1 78450 316 1

Printed and bound in Great Britain

ACKNOWLEDGEMENTS

I thank everyone, including friends, colleagues and former students, who helped bring this book into existence. Without their input, it would have been a poorer work as they helped keep me focused and relevant. In particular, I acknowledge Juhi Ahuja, Mohammed Ali Amla, Gorazd Andrejc, Tasmin Barron-Richardson, David Cheetham, Allison Coudert, Stacie Eriksson, Doug Ezzy, Jeanine Hill Fletcher, Steve James, Mohamad Imran Mohamad Taib, Akanksha Narain, Abdullah Saeed, Timothy Secret, Peter Waddell and Christina Welch.

I also thank Natalie Watson at Jessica Kingsley Publishers (JKP) for wanting to work with me again and asking me to develop this book. It brought to fruition what had been a rather aimless set of pieces I had been writing over the years, exploring the religious–atheist dialogue, into what I hope is a coherent and useful book. In addition, I thank other staff members at JKP who assisted with administration, proofreading, correcting and commenting on the manuscript as it evolved from proposal to production especially Emily Gowers, Emma Holak and Daisy Watt who have helped oversee the final stages of the process.

Whatever faults, errors and mistakes remain in the book are mine alone, and they certainly would have been multiplied were it not for the people mentioned above. I ask the reader to forgive any inadequacies and focus instead on ways that we may begin, and continue, to disagree better on the subject of religion and atheism.

CONTENTS

Note on Style 8

Introduction 9

1. Setting the Debates in Context 14

2. Books and Beliefs: Choosing and
   Interpreting Texts 36

3. Authority Figures: Jesus and the Others 57

4. God, Gods and Reality 74

5. Religions: The Good, the Bad and the Ugly 96

6. Women, Bodies and Gender 118

7. Human Animals, Non-Human Animals and
   the Universe Around Us 137

8. Living in a Religiously Diverse,
   Post-Christian and Post-Secular World 160

Further Reading 181
Index 191

NOTE ON STYLE

I capitalize 'God' when it stands for want of what may be termed a proper name or when it would traditionally be used this way. Elsewhere, I use 'god' or 'gods', and often I use the term 'deity'. What may be considered 'scriptures' (e.g. Bible, Qur'an, Bhagavad Gita) are not in italics, while other books are italicized according to the publisher's standard style. Foreign terms not generally used in English are in italics but are kept to a minimum, as I generally employ the common English-language term. For dates, I use 'BCE' (Before the Common Era) and 'CE' (Common Era), instead of 'BC' and 'AD', as this is considered more neutral terminology according to current academic convention.

INTRODUCTION

THE BOOK'S POSITION AND APPROACH

As stated by the title, this book is about better disagreement. I don't necessarily want or expect everyone to change their mind, only to become a bit more knowledgeable about the other side and its arguments (as well as understanding your own arguments better). I will try to do this by being as neutral and non-partisan as possible and simply present a discussion of the facts, making clear my own opinions only when it is useful. I do believe that atheism and religion are not simply opposite poles and locked in combat, but rather are world views which may respect and listen to each other. (I would even suggest that it may be possible to live comfortably with a foot in each camp!) If a direction for this book must be defined, perhaps it is towards an atheist, or at least agnostic, spirituality in its argument, or a form of religiosity that doesn't reject atheism.

Given that the current debates between atheism and religion are taking place mainly in a particular context, which is Western Europe and North America – not withstanding some strong atheist and humanist movements elsewhere in the world – I will focus on this context. As such, a lot of what I say will be about Christianity; however, I will also include a fair bit of discussion of Islam, as it has become such a hot topic globally and seems to me, too often, to be unfairly criticized in the crossfire. I will also discuss Buddhism, because this is often perceived to be, by many Western Buddhists at least, a form of atheist religion (they often say it is a philosophy or a way of life, not a religion) and also has a lot of appeal for a number of atheists. For instance, one well-known atheist, Sam Harris, who is often included amongst the so-called New Atheists, has spoken very appreciatively of it. Buddhism has also played a very important role, since the eighteenth century, in the rise of atheism in Europe. For many Enlightenment philosophers of that time, Buddhism provided important evidence, they believed, that humanity could form an ethical system divorced from a belief in a divine 'judge and dictator' who sent a fixed code to be followed.

In this book, I will discuss religion more than atheism, although I will certainly lay out some important and useful aspects involved in understanding atheism too. The reason for my focus on religion is because that is where much of the dispute lies. Also, it is an arena where much ignorance is exhibited – on both, the side of the atheists *and* that of the religious believers. (I do concede that the vehemence exhibited towards atheists in some parts of the world suggests there is a lot of ignorance about this position too, but at least atheists tend to know their tradition better than religious people know theirs.)

In a well-known response to Richard Dawkins' book *The God Delusion*, atheist and literary scholar Terry Eagleton issued a sharp rebuke that Dawkins very often missed his target, because he was simply ignorant about religion. He accused him of making sweeping claims and vast generalizations that were inaccurate and so easily rebutted. Even as an atheist, Eagleton claimed that he found Dawkins' book to be a poor argument against religion. While Dawkins and others have suggested that learning about religion would be a waste of their time, this is a very short-sighted stance on a number of grounds – not least is Eagleton's assertion that if you want to lay your punches accurately you need to see your target clearly. But in today's globalized world, knowing about religion is part of a rounded education. Indeed, given human history and the contemporary global context, being religiously illiterate makes one poorly equipped to have any claim to be either culturally knowledgeable or politically aware. Religious illiteracy is also dangerous if people think they can do things in a global context without understanding other people's sensibilities or beliefs. One may not agree with them, but one needs to know them.

While I *am* an academic, this book is not primarily academic in nature. As such, I avoid using footnotes and references in the text, which many people find distracting. I do, however, make reference to studies and scholars related to the points of view I am advancing. A range of suggested further reading can be found at the end of the book (in the section 'Further Reading') to look up a lot of the details and carry the study further for anyone who wishes. I realize also that especially on historical disputes there are often arguments to be made on both sides, and in terms of academic fairness and representation, I will try as far as possible to show where alternative positions exist and present the case; however, given the length of the book and the need to make it readable and not weighed down in technical discussions, these positions may not always be made in full. (Further discussion is available through the sources mentioned in the 'Further Reading' section.)

OVERVIEW

Most chapters follow a similar pattern where I first set out a historical or scholarly account of some of the debates and misunderstandings around religion and atheism, and the context from which they come. I also turn to a more personal reflection on what these debates and misunderstandings might mean today. This is where I often suggest what religious people and atheists have in common, or where they may meet for fruitful discussions. The chapters also suggest where some big disagreements can exist too. (I have no intention to paper over the cracks and pretend everyone agrees.)

Parts of the book may make for uncomfortable reading for very committed religious people who hold certain opinions as well as for very narrow-minded atheists who are convinced that religion is at the root of all of the world's problems. However, I hope that no one who sees themselves as a seeker of truth will find what I say unpalatable. As we will see, religious traditions have adapted and changed over time and are involved with the cultures, politics and society around them. This will mean, first for religious people, that what they may see as essential or treasured beliefs are actually not well grounded historically or simply have developed in particular cultural contexts, while for atheists it will show that religions can never be divorced from the world around them such that blaming some abstract entity called 'religion' for whatever evils happen in a particular age is simply naive or ill-judged. Nothing happens in the world that is not also entirely political, social and contextual.

The first chapter, 'Setting the Debates in Context', provides some general background to an intelligent debate. After showing the problems of viewing a polarized stance of religion/faith and atheism/science as separate spheres, it seeks to define what we mean by both 'religion' and 'atheism'. It concludes by looking further at the terms 'faith/belief' and 'reason' and showing that they are both aspects of human understanding.

Chapter 2, 'Books and Beliefs: Choosing and Interpreting Texts', looks at the background as to why certain texts are in the Bible as well as the attitude that religious traditions take to them. As we will see, it is not as simple as supposing that religions accept ancient texts as the final word on all things, but that rather the texts have always been read and interpreted in new ways by passing generations. We will also discuss the way that certain books become important for atheists or outside religious traditions.

The third chapter, 'Authority Figures: Jesus and the Others', deals with the lives and history of figures like Jesus, Muhammad and the Buddha. As we will see, the history is not simply about their lives but also the changing ways they have been understood and related to over time, both inside and outside of their traditions. We will also consider the kind of ways they are seen to have authority and what significance that has.

Chapter 4 considers 'God, Gods and Reality' and looks at the variety of beliefs which exist and the credibility of such beliefs in both historical and contemporary contexts. In particular, it examines what is often termed the problem of evil: Can an all-loving and all-powerful God allow suffering and evil in the world? It also looks at the place of atheism as a world view in relation to various religions.

Chapter 5, 'Religions: The Good, the Bad and the Ugly', gives an overview of some contested history of various religions and their positive and negative sides. Clearly, religions have been involved with – and have justified – violence, war and conflict, although many adherents, both today and in the past, have claimed that the essential message of their tradition is peace. (Certainly many pacifist and anti-nuclear campaigns have been led by, or had strong input from, religious groups.) I put forth that either blaming religion for the bad and saying the good is not down to religion, or just praising the good and saying the bad does not represent religion, is not an adequate answer. How to deal with this legacy today is also discussed, as is the question as to what extent atheism has, or has not, been involved in such problems.

Chapter 6 deals with the vexed question of 'Women, Bodies and Gender', which has always been a big area of contention. Are religions against women and sexuality, and responsible for negative attitudes to the body? I argue that certainly most religions do not have a good track record, but also that to claim *all* religion is either against or for something, is too simplistic. Indeed, sexism seems to permeate many spheres of life, as we will discuss.

The seventh chapter, 'Human Animals, Non-Human Animals and the Universe Around Us', deals with a variety of disputes, or perceived disputes, between science and religion, as well as touching on environmental concerns. We look at the historical and theoretical aspects of the disputes. It is not directly about discussing animals, though, and I hope the reader will realize the words here refer in large part to questions raised by evolution such as: Are we related to monkeys and are simply human animals?

The final chapter (Chapter 8) is entitled 'Living in a Religiously Diverse, Post-Christian and Post-Secular World' and addresses a number of factors in our contemporary world. Amongst these factors are what is called the secularization thesis, which saw sociologists in the twentieth century claim that religion was dying and would disappear by the end of that century if not long into the twenty-first century, whereas contemporary contexts suggest that religion is resurgent and certainly not going to die out any time soon. As such, how do we cope with this? We also address religious diversity, which has been with us for a long time but means today that we live in increasingly diverse and multifaith societies. So how do both religious and non-religious people conceptualize this and work with it? My conclusion to this chapter is 'What can Christians, atheists and others share today?' and provides something of a conclusion to the whole book suggesting that religion and atheism need not be at war and can actually live harmoniously alongside each other, and each can even learn from the other.

1

SETTING THE DEBATES IN CONTEXT

INTRODUCTION

This is a book about being human. It is written both for atheists who want to gain a more sympathetic understanding of religion and for religious people who want to gain a more sympathetic understanding of atheism. However, it is also written for atheists who want to understand atheism better and for religious people who want to understand religion better. It is often assumed, or argued, that atheism and religious belief are opposed or antagonistic; indeed, atheists and believers are often in argument. Nevertheless, I do not see them as necessarily opposed and seek to find common points and areas of meeting.

My aim may sound ambitious, and I'm sure that a lot of people will start off reading this book thinking it sounds crazy, kooky or just downright dishonest: 'You can't find common ground between religion and atheism: they are opposed; religious people rely on faith, atheists and scientists rely on reason and evidence'. If this viewpoint makes sense to you, however, you really need to read this book, and if it doesn't, then I think you may like this book and benefit from reading it. If you're in the former group, then I think you may benefit even more. Just to set out a little of what I mean, I'll give a few examples.

A lot of rhetoric in the religion–atheism debates uses very polarized language: atheists, rationalists and scientists are often categorized into one group, whereas believers, theists and religious people are in another camp. Certainly, some prominent atheists, like Paul Kurtz (1925–2012), have opposed such language, but it is prominent in the debates today. Particularly, people say that science is about evidence and reason, and religion is about (blind) faith. Even intelligent, well-educated and otherwise rational proponents on either side make such claims; however, let's see if this kind of language even makes any sense, and to do so, I'll take four examples:

1. The history of science will show you various things; amongst them is the fact that many of the most important figures in its development were religious. For a few examples (in historical order):

    - William of Ockham (1285–1347), famous for Ockham's razor (see Chapter 7), was a Franciscan friar.

    - Taqi al-Din Muhammad ibn Ma'ruf al-Shami as-Asadi (1526–1585) was a Muslim astronomer and mathematician, working in the Ottoman Empire, whose astronomical observations exceeded those of his European contemporaries like Tycho Brahe (1546–1601) (see Chapter 7).

    - Isaac Newton (1642–1727) was a Christian and an alchemist.

    - Albert Einstein (1879–1955) was a religious person (even if not conventionally so) from a Jewish background.

    - These are only four examples, but as the history of science shows, far from being exceptions they are very much representative. So, if we have 'rational scientists' as one category and 'faith-based, anti-rational religious people' in another category, how do we explain this?

2. A number of studies suggest that science does not in itself lead people to atheism. One survey examined students of which majors were most likely to be atheists. If physical science and religion are opposed, then we'd surely expect the hard-science subjects to top the list of most atheists. However, this clearly isn't so: the social sciences have the most atheists, followed by

the humanities. By contrast, most hard-science subjects were pretty much middle of the list, while philosophy was another strong shower in the majority atheist camp. Another survey looked at changes in religious belief during students' degrees. Again, it was not studying the physical sciences that led to atheism; rather, students of the social sciences and humanities were most likely to *lose* their faith. Study of the biological or physical sciences had no effect on this. Clearly, studying science itself does not incline one to atheism more than many other forms of study.

- Such studies contradict the claims of biologist and atheist Jerry Coyne, that studying or practising science leads to atheism; however, his selected and mainly USA examples may not be representative. Studies have looked at practising scientists and whether they tended to believe in God. While the majority of scientists in the West don't believe in God, and certainly studies of USA scientists suggest that they are far less likely than the general population to believe in God (with certain elite groups, as Coyne argues, being most atheistically inclined), this is not the whole picture. A recent Pew Research Centre study in the USA showed that while only 33% of scientists believed in a personal God, against 41% who did not, a further 18% believed in some form of higher power or spirit, making the majority what we may term 'religious' in some sense. Moreover, 7% either didn't know or didn't answer.

- Interestingly, studies have shown that in Taiwan and Hong Kong, scientists are more religious than the population at large. This may reflect the way religion, and also science, is envisaged in those countries. However, it is clear that polarizing claims about religion and science, or that science makes people more atheist, simply don't stand up when a wide range of evidence is considered. One can very easily be a Christian (or Muslim, Jew, Buddhist, Sikh and so forth) *and* a scientist. Of course, this does not show that a conflict does not exist at some level, but we cannot say that science leads to atheism without abusing the evidence. (We will discuss this further in Chapter 7.)

3. The history of human thought and culture is littered with examples of deeply rational religious people in every field from philosophy to the arts, from music to cultural studies. If atheists and religious people are opposed, then maybe atheists need to dismiss the work of Mozart and Bach, Michelangelo and Leonardo da Vinci, or works like the Shiva *Nataraja* (Lord of the Dance) and Chinese or Japanese landscape paintings or gardens – all inspired by religion. But contrarily, should religious believers dismiss the (atheist inspired?) works of figures like Bizet and van Gogh? Clearly, this would be pretty absurd. But what is not absurd is recognizing that every human culture is deeply underpinned by religious belief. Therefore, understanding the world's heritage of music, art, architecture, poetry and philosophy means appreciating and coming to grips with the beliefs that have underpinned it. It is a legacy continued by both atheists and religious people who create the art and culture around us; as such, dismissing atheism alienates one from some of the most creative aspects of the contemporary world. Today, both atheism and religion can claim deeply intelligent, moral and sophisticated people who shape the world in which we live.

4. Some people simply do not fit comfortably into either atheist or religious boxes, at least as the debates are commonly portrayed (caricatured). For instance, Thomas Paine's (1737–1809) *Age of Reason* (1794) is looked to by atheists because of quotes like this:

   • Whenever we read the obscene stories, the voluptuous debaucheries, the cruel and torturous executions, the unrelenting vindictiveness with which more than half the Bible is filled, it would be more consistent that we called it the word of a demon…'

   • However, in that text Paine clearly stated he was not an atheist: 'I believe in one God, and no more; and I hope for happiness beyond this life'. (He is what is termed a 'deist', an idea discussed in Chapter 4.)

• In Asia, some look to Confucius (c. 551–479 BCE) as a foundational non-religious figure, especially citing his words

'We have not yet learned to serve men. How can we serve the gods and the spirits?' (Analects XI.12) as indicating that he had no interest in a spiritual or supernatural world, and certainly he does not discourse about gods. However, Confucius saw the world as controlled by *Tian* (literally 'sky', but meaning in many contexts 'heaven'). It seems unlikely Confucius envisaged *Tian* as a personal deity but rather as a transcendent reality. Likewise, as we will discuss throughout the book, some people may feel the need for some form of 'spiritual' sense even if not accepting a traditional form of belief in a deity or any established religious tradition.

I hope you will accept that these four points at least indicate that the world is not split (at least not inherently) into two opposing camps: rationalist/atheist/scientific and faith-based/belief-based/anti-scientific. Such a stance is simply ignorant of history and the contemporary world. Nevertheless, I won't deny that there are those in both camps who see things this way, and certainly many religious people today perceive science as in some ways opposed to their religious beliefs and faith, and will distinguish faith and reason as two ways of approaching the world (at least in certain contexts). Likewise, many atheists are often in a contrary position, and to some degree the history of the development of modern atheism comes from a context that gives some credence to such a view. My argument, however, is that things need not be this way; indeed, they are not 'naturally' this way. I even assert that to some degree the perception, or reality, of hostility between those who see themselves in one of these two opposing camps is down to 'bad religion' and 'bad atheism' (although there can be good reasons to see tensions or dissonances, but not wholesale dismissal of the other), or else a poor understanding of history, theology, culture and critical thinking.

We must also address another misunderstanding. So far we have dealt with a stereotype that religious people may be irrational, while atheists may be rational, and certainly across a lot of Europe it is religious people who feel the need to defend their credibility from a secular world. Elsewhere, however, a stereotype is that atheists are immoral, while religious people make up the moral fibre of society. More than this, we must not forget that in a good number of countries atheists face not just condemnation but also violence and death, a trend that seems to be increasing in places such as Bangladesh. Less extreme than such violence, in parts of the USA and elsewhere, atheists find themselves on the defensive, even persecuted, because they are perceived to destroy morals and society. The experience of Europe, or places like Australia and New Zealand, where a largely secular society exists, shows that we can't give credence to such views; atheists can be good citizens and moral people. Indeed, the behaviour of many religious people and traditions down the ages certainly should give anyone pause for thought if they think that religion has some sort of monopoly on morality. It has even been suggested to me by one person with a religious leadership position that if atheists can find their own moral compass from within themselves, rather than relying on external rules and regulations, as many religious people may seem to do (but it is equally a stereotype to say all religious people don't have morality without texts and guidelines), then they may be equally spiritual, if not more so, than many people who claim a religious identity. Of course, this may not be a label with which atheists would be happy, but it does show a different perspective.

In the rest of this chapter I will set out a bit more groundwork which will help orientate us through the rest of the book. First, I will address the question of what the term 'religion' means before asking what we mean by 'atheism'. Afterwards, I will discuss the terms 'faith/belief' and 'reason', and ask if they really represent two different approaches to the world.

WHAT IS RELIGION?

Most people are pretty certain what they mean by 'religion'. In day-to-day usage it is fairly clear. It may come as something of a surprise, therefore, to know that since the 1960s there has been a debate in Religious Studies (the academic and non-confessional study of religion) over whether the term 'religion' is actually meaningful. If you assume that there is a clear area called 'religion', which is somehow different from everything else, this may seem strange, but I will explain some factors that make identifying religion hard. Some problems of definition are addressed in Box 1.1, while I will proceed to discuss the variety of things we call 'religion'.

Box 1.1

Defining religion

It is very hard to find a definition that only fits all those things we commonly call 'religion' and doesn't include the things we don't. A dictionary definition may say something like 'a belief in a God or Gods'. This seems straightforward, but what about traditions like Buddhism, which do not have any central deity? We normally call it a religion, but it doesn't fit our central idea. We may then say that it involves belief in some form of transcendent or supernatural power, force, energy or knowledge. It may not be clear, though, what we mean by 'transcendent' or 'supernatural', but let us say it is something which cannot be seen, touched or otherwise perceived and acts outside the normal course of human and physical laws. Once again, though, we find that lots of things actually refer to something like this. A classic example is Marxism, which tells us that history is moving towards the inevitable victory of the proletariat. Marxism, however, is in many forms avowedly atheist; Karl Marx (1818–1883) himself described religion as the 'opium of the people'. However, it relies upon a force which is entirely outside our normal sources of knowledge. Does that make it a religion? Some may think that Marxism is largely outmoded and an old theory, but the same actually applies to today's dominant socio-economic model of capitalism. We are told that the economy is run by 'market forces' and that this mysterious power (unseen, unknowable except through what we are told by the 'high priests' of economics) is what we should trust and will ensure that all works out.

It may be objected that neither capitalism nor Marxism actually refer to forces which operate outside the world or cosmos – rather, they are inside it – but many religions would make the same claim. Pagans often see the divine as something within the universe or related to the earth, a belief called pantheism (though many Pagans are polytheists, some are atheists and some hold other views). It is hard to know why we should trust and believe in one set of invisible forces and not another. Again, some may suggest that religion is about a total and guiding ideology which rules the whole of somebody's life, but this ignores the fact that most people who subscribe to a religion do not behave that way. It also ignores many other world views which provide a justification for what people do, whether it be some form of nationalism, political ideology or even devotion to some philosophy or the pursuit of knowledge. In terms of the way they operate and provide forms of validation for those within them, it is hard to define how religion differs from many other world views.

All the things we call 'religions' are actually very different. For instance, although those religions familiar to most people in the Western world (i.e. Christianity, Islam and Judaism) share some features, such as a supreme creator deity, a sacred text(s) and forms of belief, they also have many differences, as do the other religions of the world. Judaism, for instance, is often termed an orthopraxy, which means that it is more concerned with correct practice rather than correct belief (orthodoxy), which characterizes much contemporary Christianity. Buddhism, as mentioned, does not have a creator deity. It is unclear whether Confucianism has any form of belief in any transcendent reality, as one of its main foundational thinkers, a philosopher called Xunzi (third century BCE), seemed to invoke the natural world to explain the way things are. This is not to deny that others, like Mencius (c. 372–289 BCE), had what we may term a more spiritual world view, but arguably this was about self-perfection and involved no deity either (scholars are divided on the question).

That which we have come to term Hinduism is often seen as a form of polytheism, that is, it has many gods, although many believe these are just manifestations of a single divine source. But, importantly for us, as the traditions that surround it codified themselves into six orthodox philosophical schools, it includes at least one which denies any form of divine reality, that is, it is atheist. As such, one can be an atheist Hindu and sit very comfortably within the historically defined bounds of that 'religion'. (It may be that Hinduism does not refer to a single system as many have argued; however, no religious tradition is defined by a single point of view and all are very diverse.)

To sum up some of the diversity of the things we often call religions (with a few points I haven't yet mentioned), some have a deity or deities, some do not; some have sacred texts, some do not; some insist on certain forms of belief or doctrine, some do not; some invoke some form of transcendent or supernatural force, some do not; some require particular clothing, some do not. Quite simply, when people make sweeping claims about 'religion is…', or 'all religious people are…', it is not clear what that could possibly mean given the diversity of traditions we typically call religions.

Now, because much atheist thought has developed in a Western European and North American context, it is fair to say that actually what is often meant when claims about 'religion' are made actually means Christianity. Sometimes this is extended to include Judaism and Islam; today Islam is often invoked, or even made out to be worse than any other religion – a view that seems to be held by prominent atheists such as Richard Dawkins, Sam Harris and the late Christopher Hitchens. (I will return to issues surrounding negative attitudes to Islam, which are often these days summed up by the term 'Islamophobia', in due course.)

Again, particularly for North American atheists, a lot of the polemic is often addressed at the kinds of evangelical or fundamentalist Protestantism that are particularly vocal in that context. It may then be assumed that this represents all Christianity, and by extension all forms of religion, which allows a blanket condemnation. It may be that there are common points to many of the things we call religion, and that some forms of bad or irrational behaviour can be seen replicated in many places. However, as I suggested above, to go from a strong dislike – which may be well founded – of certain forms of religion, and then suggest that this extends to all religion, and importantly all religious people, seems rather sweeping. If all that religion has produced is somehow tainted with irrationality, this leads to the absurd point I raised earlier that we must condemn figures such as Shakespeare and Milton, Rumi and Homer, as much of their work was shaped by their religious worlds. Of course, showing that religions are deeply involved in the development of art, culture and our ideas about reason is not in itself a defence of religion against atheism; this involvement does not show that they are right. Importantly, though, when condemnation of religion becomes condemnation of religious *people*, and when condemnation of one form of religion becomes condemnation of *all* forms of religion, we see huge, sweeping generalizations at work. Of course, the same is equally true when religious polemics attack atheism and all atheists as corrupt, immoral or lacking culture. This is something to be developed as we proceed.

WHAT IS ATHEISM?

The kind of debates that scholars have had over whether 'religion' is a meaningful word or whether it actually refers to a unified and coherent set of traditions has not occurred to the same degree in relation to atheism. However, this does not mean that atheism is a simple word either, nor that it is readily understood. Rather than go into the history of the term, I raise three points about it: First, posing the question of whether atheism is simply negative and dependent on theism (belief in God) or religion. Second, saying something about the complexity of atheist traditions. Third, addressing issues about morality and ideas as foundations for atheism.

Is atheism simply negative and dependent on theism?

The construction of the word 'atheism' − as 'a-theism' − makes it seem as though it is a world view whose sole, or major, focus is the denial of God. In philosophical terms this is what would be called the etymological fallacy, that is, the idea that the root or origin of a word tells us what it 'really means' or its 'proper usage'. Atheism can be seen as a world view which simply has no relation to theism. But, as all societies have been predominantly religious throughout history, those that hold a different viewpoint are termed in relation to that societal norm. Within a Western context, we hence get the term 'atheism', and certainly much of the atheist case has been made, historically, through a denial of, or arguments against, the existence of God. (We come back to some of this in later chapters, especially Chapter 4.) It is worth noting, though, that seeing what we term 'religious traditions' and 'atheist traditions' as constructed against each other is not the only story. As noted, the Hindu family of religions has come to define six orthodox schools of philosophy, at least one of which is avowedly atheist or materialist. Seeing forms of atheism as simply being against God or theism reflects a very Western world view. In Chinese or Indian contexts, we would see a different conception.

In the contemporary context, a case for understanding atheism as an outworking of a naturalist world system can equally well be made, as opposed to it being necessarily a rejection of theism or religion. Indeed if, at some future point, societies exist where nobody, or very few, believe in God, then it would be possible to be an atheist without even giving a second thought to what it may be against. In fact, if societies had evolved in different ways, we would perhaps speak of religious people as 'aphysicalists' − those who deny that the physical world as experienced directly through the senses, is simply all there is.

This would not make religion parasitic on such a view, nor negative, although it might also make its arguments primarily *against* such a world view. Atheism, therefore, need not simply be seen as negative, or a denial of religion. This is perhaps shown more by some terms, such as humanist (discussed below), freethinker or sceptic, which certain atheists prefer.

The complexity of atheist traditions

Atheist world views have existed in many different societies at different times and have been expressed in different ways. As we noted, the Confucian philosopher Xunzi was an atheist. Against common world views which offered prayers or rituals for rain, he asked, 'If you pray, why did it rain?' His answer: because it was going to rain anyway. Regardless of prayers and rituals, or no prayers and rituals, nature simply follows its own course: there is no supernatural intervention. Likewise, ancient India and Greece also developed forms of atheist thought; these, however, can be complex. Socrates (c. 470–399 BCE) was killed, the records suggest, for denying the city gods, and this has led some to see him as an atheist. However, it is not clear that he was atheist in the sense in which it would be seen today, and another charge levelled at him was that he introduced new gods. Nevertheless, more clearly atheist thought existed in figures like Anaximander (610–546 BCE), Democritus (460–370 BCE) and Thales (c. sixth century BCE), and it is likely that atheists have existed in pretty much all cultures. However, to express atheism has often been dangerous, and within a Western context it was really only expressed from around the time known as the Enlightenment (a period generally dated around the seventeenth to the eighteenth centuries, although sometimes narrowly to 1720–1780) where some locate the modern traditions of atheism. Earlier figures like Giulio Cesare Vanini (1585–1619), who were openly and polemically atheist, are mainly isolated individuals, and his execution for atheism and blasphemy may suggest why.

In the modern West, atheism has evolved from various influences. The growth of atheism in the eighteenth and nineteenth centuries was partly scientific (see Chapter 7), but more often it was either historical, as it was realized that the biblical text contained errors and inconsistencies, or philosophical, based around moral repugnance at religion (see Chapters 2, 4 and 5). Another influence – one which gives a name to one strand of atheism – is Humanism, which emphasizes putting centre stage both the human being and a positive, value-affirming life. The term itself goes back to the Renaissance, when it arose as a Christian philosophy looking to classical Greek and Roman sources, although seemingly it had derived more directly from Islamic sources. For atheist Humanists, this classical tradition becomes a source of atheist inspiration.

A turn to the philosophies of Buddhism and Confucianism was also an influence, particularly in the Enlightenment period. Many interpreted these traditions/religions as atheist world views. Importantly, with both Confucius (c. 551–479 BCE) and the Buddha (c. fifth century BCE) being seen as figures who had developed an ethical system as human beings without divine influence, this was taken as evidence that morality could not just be found but also positively extolled without a set of rules given by a deity – an important argument against Christian polemics. Atheism draws, therefore, from many sources and strands, and is not simply about the denial of the type of God found in the so-called Abrahamic religions (Judaism, Christianity and Islam), but rather has drawn from different philosophical and scientific currents, and developed across many different cultures. Some people who define themselves as atheist see their rationale as a modern Western one that is scientific or philosophical, but non-Western and non-modern world views have also developed atheist traditions. It is important to emphasize this last point as sometimes people suggest it is simply a modern or Western standpoint.

Morality and ideas as foundations for atheism

We have discussed so far some of the ideas which may underlie an atheist world view, and terms like 'freethinker' or 'sceptic' may reinforce the notion that it is primarily intellectual. However, atheism is equally, if not more, about moral and social ideas. Revolt against what is seen as an unjust and despotic God, or flight from the corruption and cruelty of a religious institution, have been historically – and still quite possibly today – far more common reasons for people to become atheist than from careful consideration of the facts and evidence. Within a reasoned world view, atheism can carry with it many moral and social perspectives, which are often reflected in Humanism. Notably, as Michael Ruse has argued, the kind of natural-law theory found in traditional Catholic Christian thinkers like Saint Thomas Aquinas (1225–1274), can be supportive of atheism, as it supposes that morals are not something external that we need to be given, but rather are innate and part of the natural order, something which would also resonate with evolutionary perspectives about how we have adapted as a species. Indeed, we may note that the beliefs of figures like Aquinas and others, that ethical values are the common norms of humanity, supplies something of an answer to Hitchens' polemical challenge for someone to show him a moral act that could only exist in religion and not be developed by an atheist. In the Catholic Christian tradition, at least, a claim is made that we would not expect to find one – of course, this contradicts some other rhetorical claims that religion is the source of morality. (We take up a related theme in Chapter 8.)

FAITH VERSUS REASON?

Another typical point of contention is the idea that religion is about 'faith' or 'belief' and that science and atheism are about 'reason'. As I have argued above, the idea that we find 'religious people' who fit into one camp and 'freethinkers' who fit into the other is simply absurd. Nevertheless, it is repeated over and over again. In debates, atheists know they can always get a little cheer by invoking this ploy, while religious spokespeople can see accusations of lack of faith as a put-down against those who fail to see their point of view. Actually, I do not think that faith/belief and reason are totally different spheres – we all use both, which is part of being human. However, as I have seen very intelligent atheists say that they do not have 'belief', I had better explain. (Of course, religious believers may also say that their 'faith' gives them some form of 'higher knowledge' or superior standpoint, and this is not justified either.)

Let's look at a very basic definition first. What does it mean to have faith in something, or to believe something? It means to take something as true, which you don't have immediate evidence for or even cannot verify. This could be either rational, irrational or arational (more on this later). I am not talking about religious faith here; it is common or garden everyday stuff. I go into work one day and put my sandwiches in the fridge first thing in the morning. Why do I go back at lunchtime to look for them? I go because I believe they are there. I have faith in my colleagues not to steal them. I have a belief that those bits of bread are still where I left them. I may not have seen them for several hours, but we do make acts of faith like this (based on reasonable assumptions). It may be objected that we could test this, so it is not about faith or belief; nevertheless, I would argue that I have just used those words in ways which everyone understands, and it is therefore meaningful. It is what people mean by using those terms. However, let me give more examples: Suppose you are in a relationship with somebody and you come to believe that this person is in love with you. Would this be faith, belief or knowledge? The other person may say they love you, but people can lie. They may perform very kind actions, but maybe they are just being nice or don't want to hurt you. The relationship may be long-lasting and solid, which may provide evidence for your beliefs. However, at what stage can you say you can become certain – that you can know, rather than simply have a belief, that the other person loves you? If you are cynical, you may say never, but most people would think that point would come, which suggests that before that moment, it was a belief. You may wish to say, assuming you wanted to argue, that being a rational person you didn't *have* a belief – you merely held a working hypothesis that the other person loved you. All you were doing was conducting an experiment to see if they really loved you and whether you could have enough knowledge. Even, you might suggest, you may simply have a more solid hypothesis because every hypothesis is subject to change if the circumstances change. If you take this point of view, I would wonder, however, what kind of relationship it was, and I may even suggest that you needed some counselling. In everyday life we come to have belief and faith in many things.

On a more philosophical note, René Descartes (1596–1650) observed that almost every belief we have could be doubted. What if we are asleep and only imagine ourselves to be awake? That would mean this chair I am sitting on is not really here at all. A similar thought experiment is found in an ancient Chinese book, the Zhuangzi (c. fourth century BCE; often spelt Chuang Tse or Chuang Tzu), and the general concept will be familiar to anyone who has seen the film *The Matrix*. In other words, what if our reality is not quite what we think it is? When we are dreaming we are not aware that we are dreaming, and so how do we test that we are not in some illusion, dream or hallucination right now? Descartes' answer was to invoke God; however, it is an answer not open to the atheist. We may suggest – indeed, I would say with good reason – that sheer common sense and the need to operate in the world in a rational way means we cannot live like this. Nevertheless, on a day-to-day level we do operate on a basis of certain beliefs, or even faith. When I cross the road at the crossing point I have faith that the car will slow down and stop, but maybe the driver will have a heart attack and *not* stop; or when I lean back on my chair, I have a belief that it will support me, but weakened by overuse it may suddenly collapse.

My point is that faith/belief (I am using the terms fairly interchangeably here as is common in normal daily usage rather than in any technical way) is not something only found amongst religious people and not atheists; we all, on a day-to-day basis, have faith/belief in similar ways. It also suggests that our beliefs are not simply irrational; instead, we can have faith in something for a reason. Of course, it may be objected both that religious faith is different and that science also requires faith (see Box 1.2). Let's explore both of these viewpoints, but first allow me to face another possible objection, which is that my language of faith/belief here could equally be replaced by words like 'expect' or 'assume'. So I could expect the car to stop, or assume the chair will hold my weight. Certainly, we could have this discussion without invoking the terms belief or faith. Nevertheless, my point is that whatever we call it, we operate, on a day-to-day basis, supposing that things about which we may not be fully certain, or simply cannot investigate in detail, will happen in ways we expect. As I will argue further below, such suppositions or beliefs are a natural part of what we do; therefore, religious belief is not some strange and distinct sphere or human behaviour, but rather is related to things we do elsewhere in life. This should become clearer in my examples below. As such, the terms are not essential; as Shakespeare put it, 'A rose by any other name would smell as sweet'. Likewise, it does not matter what we call our behaviour; rather, the way humans operate is what should concern us. Certainly, if we were not communicating in

English, especially in non-European languages, we would likely find that the words we are using would hold very different connotations.

First, is religious faith different from the faith I have that somebody loves me? Arguably it is. I can see my loved one, interact with them on a daily basis and see their actions and hear their words. Of course, many religious people will claim experiences of the divine that mirror this, but generally it is not considered something that is part of the physical world in the same way. Does this, however, make it quantifiably different? I suggest two thought experiments: First, suppose you live in twelfth-century Europe, and so you live in a world where everybody you know is Christian and believes in God. (You may have met or heard of Muslims and Jews, and even heretics, but that does not challenge the basic narrative.) You have a wonderful inner experience of something that seems to go beyond anything you can describe or imagine. You, your relatives, your friends – indeed, your entire society – tells you that this is an experience of God; therefore, you have a firm and unshakable belief in God. Is this an irrational belief for the person to hold? Or, to put the question another way, would it be irrational of them *not* to believe in God? We even may ask: Why is this belief different from their belief that their childhood sweetheart loves them? The person, I suggest, is acting fully in accord with the knowledge, evidence and experiences available to them. This, presumably, is rational? This, of course, is not the same as saying it is a true belief, but it is based on the only premises they have.

Let us now consider a second example: Susan has always been in love with Donald. They have been going out for many years, and Donald enjoys the lifestyle that Susan's good job provides. He is always kind and loving towards her, and they seem happy. One day, though, Susan arrives home early and sees Donald kissing another woman in the street. When she questions him, he tells her that this was a very old friend he hadn't seen in ages, and they were just saying goodbye. Over the next few weeks the phone rings, but the person at the other end doesn't speak and just hangs up if Susan answers the phone. Donald has to go out more, claiming that he is meeting his friends, although sometimes Susan finds that he wasn't actually with those friends at the time he said. He also seems a bit more distant from her and seems to have secrets he didn't have before.

Nevertheless, Donald is hunky, and Susan is besotted with him. She trusts him and still believes that he loves her. Even when he tells her that he wants to leave her for someone else, Susan still believes this can't be true and that deep down he really loves her. Is Susan irrational to believe that he still loves her – or that he *ever* loved her?

These two little thought experiments ask us to do at least three things:

- to ask when belief is rational and what kind of things make it so

- to imagine what it is like to believe something for which we don't have proof – indeed, for which there may even be good reasons *not* to believe but which nevertheless we are very strongly emotionally inclined to believe

- to ask what social and psychological context make a belief rational or irrational, where we act in accord with the evidence which we have.

I suggest that actually there is no clear distinction between religious belief and pretty much any other form of belief. This is, indeed, not just my claim but is the result of many studies in psychology and the social sciences. There is no single clear factor, or even cluster of factors, that can be identified that separates religious belief from other forms of belief. As mentioned, scholars find it hard to get a working definition that clearly demarcates all those things we commonly call religion from many other types of world view, whether these be nationalisms, Nazism, Marxism or whatever. The way we make and maintain any form of world view or ideology seems to have very deep similarities across any sphere. Indeed, when sociologists or psychologists examine religion from the approach of social formation, identity creation or any other factor, there is nothing that marks religion apart, excepting that is our common tendency to label certain things as religious and other things as not religious. We must note the following: religions historically manifest in different ways, so any distinction between the 'religious sphere' and other spheres of life will reflect the observer's cultural norms and values. In belief or anything else there is not some special sphere of 'religious' belief that is different from what human beings do in other areas of life. Of course, many religious traditions will insist that faith in their tradition is something special, but any such claim ultimately rests in a realm which can't be tested.

I can sense some potential objections, which I will phrase as responses to my first thought experiment:

- It may be said that we don't live in the twelfth century, so while being religious may have been rational then, it is not rational now, so religious faith shows that the people who have it are irrational.

- Whatever century we are talking about, religious faith means believing in something that cannot be seen, touched or otherwise sensed through the normal processes; therefore, it is different.

- Religious faith is fixed and unchangeable, and therefore different from other types of faith, as it is not open to new evidence.

First, yes, it is quite clear that we are in a different century, when, in many places, religion is no longer as predominant as it once was. Furthermore, we live after Darwin and the rise of many sciences which shift the balance of arguments (see Chapter 7). Indeed, if you had lived in the twelfth century, being an atheist may have been irrational (it would mean assuming that the whole society around you was wrong, that the most educated and cleverest people of the age were wrong, and little evidence existed to explain the world in any other way), whereas today both are active and reasonable world views. Consider the following points (which are covered in more detail in Chapters 4 and 8):

- Many people are brought up in social conditions and communities where religion is normal and mainstream, as such, believing in it is just something they do.

- It is clear that still today many rational and well-educated people – scientists, lawyers, engineers, doctors and so on – are religious, and clearly, they are not just strange lunatics out of touch with the world; therefore, it is possible to be rational and religious. (People may, of course, bracket out rationality in this sphere, but I will come to that shortly.)

- People claim to have experiences which ground their faith, that is, strong and powerful emotional reactions which exert huge power on people's minds. Whether the experiences are based in some divine reality, or not, does not change the point that they are experienced, and – like love (I come to this again below) – affect what we think, feel and understand.

- A number of evolutionary theorists suggest that religion is hardwired into us and has evolved as a useful evolutionary tool; as such, being religious is an innate part of being human.

The last argument is often used to show that religion is not divine, just part of the process of natural selection. However, if correct, it does show that being religious is something built into us and quite 'natural'; therefore, portraying religious people as weird, aberrant or strange ignores the fact that they are behaving in a very normal way (see Chapter 8). This does not, of course, make their beliefs true or even morally justified; however, they are not simply fantasies or fairy tales that can dissolve into thin air, but rather are ingrained cultural and evolutionary ways of thinking and being.

Second, to some extent, religious faith is often in something you can't perceive; however, has anyone ever 'seen' love, the Marxist force of history or market forces (to use some examples invoked above)? People believe in a lot of things not available to the senses. Anyone who believes that their country is the great Motherland and the greatest country on earth, and that they should be willing to die to defend it, is investing in a lot of narratives based on subjective and intangible ideas. Certainly, for all of these things, people will say they have experience of how they work in the world, or are experienced in their lives. This is exactly what religious people do as well, whether it is the love shown by other believers, seeming miracles or unexplained events, and so forth. Atheists may wish to argue that many of these things can be seen elsewhere or can potentially be explained in other ways; however, the same would go for the grounding narratives and experiences for any other ideology, world view or even the experience of love. What goes on in the head of a religious person is not some peculiar area of 'religious sensibility' but rather part of the general aspect of behaviour and belief formation that happens in everyday life.

While I am directly critiquing an atheist argument that religion is somehow deviant and different, the defence is actually not one which necessarily supports the standard religious defence either – advocates of both standpoints often make bad arguments. Indeed, part of my argument is that religious belief is not a special realm that should be treated differently, which many religious apologists would claim. Rather, religious belief is similar in almost all ways to other forms of belief in terms of how it is attained, maintained or lost.

Third, I agree that many religious people stick to opinions and beliefs that may seem to go against the evidence presented to them. However, this again is not some peculiar religious form of activity but rather something quite normal in human behaviour. Also, as with other forms of belief, it is open to change: religious people do become atheists, or convert to another religion, or become agnostics, and even change their religious position within one tradition. Studies of identity and patterns of belief show quite clearly, whatever the form of belief, that those beliefs that are most significant to somebody's identity are very hard to change or dislodge. Even on a day-to-day basis we all know that if somebody has a preformed opinion on something, it is hard to change their minds; we tend, as humans, to stick to what we already know and require more evidence to dislodge an established belief than to initiate one. Of course, if we tend to be more open-minded and genuinely practise intellectual humility, we can be less rigid and more open to new ideas. However, there is no study of which I am aware that shows that religious beliefs or 'religious people' actually are any different from other forms of beliefs or people. Certainly, in as far as people invest these beliefs with a sense of 'ultimacy' (divine truth) or absolute centrality to their lives (i.e. they define their identity primarily by reference to their religion), they become very central and hard to dislodge; but this is not a different case from convinced nationalists or Marxists or advocates of any other ideology. None of this shows that either side is right or wrong; my main argument here is that all humans operate in quite similar ways, whether religious or non-religious.

Returning to a point noted above, it may be suggested that religious believers selectively suspend their rationality when they come to religious faith – they make a leap into irrationality and depart from their normal rational behaviour. Indeed, some religious thinkers will make this claim, and the nineteenth-century philosopher Søren Kierkegaard (1813–1855) is one such example who is often seen as supporting a 'leap of faith'. However, I suggest this is too simple: some people can believe things for good reasons, and elsewhere we can believe things for bad reasons; however, almost all of us at some point will 'suspend our rationality' in areas like love and relationships, politics, nationalism, devotion to a sports team or religion. My thought experiment on Susan and Donald made this point: we can probably all recognize people who have believed what they want 'against the odds'. But the fact that some religious belief may involve a suspension of rationality does not mean that all religious belief involves this, nor that it is unique to religion, or irrational (at least in any special way). Philosophers may term some things like this as arational, that is, we make decisions based on reasons but supported by emotion and some sense of judgement, which is not strictly using reason. We cannot prove either way if God exists or not (though, as we will see in Chapter 4, it may not be clear what we mean by the term 'God' or whether the claimed reality of many religions can be spoken of in this way). As such, to be a believer or atheist perhaps is always arational, but some beliefs can be better founded, some can be irrational and some can be rational. (Just to be clear, I am not saying that since we don't know, it's no better than a 50/50 either way, or that all forms of religious belief, or even all forms of atheism, are equally adequate or rational: some forms of belief are clearly more rational and accord better with the evidence or logic, as Richard Dawkins has argued.)

Box 1.2

Does science need faith?

A contested question is whether scientific belief requires 'faith', a debate that depends on how we use and define the word 'faith' or 'belief', and often each party simply talks past each other. So, to set the scene, let us first explain what each side means on their own terms. I will ask you to set aside your own position for a second and try to see what the other side wants to say:

> Position A: Science is based on experimentation and hypothesis. In general, the scientific method works by

a hypothesis and setting up experiments for this with suitable control samples and other precautions to ensure its accuracy. Hypotheses that pass more tests become more solid or sure, and may even become more or less certain, while hypotheses which fail the tests are discarded or modified. As such, no belief is required. You do not believe an initial hypothesis until it is tested and do not place belief (untested knowing) on any hypothesis, while acknowledging that every experiment is capable of casting doubt on any hypothesis such that it may need to be abandoned or modified; therefore, the whole process is belief-free.

Position B: Science proceeds by testing hypotheses, as described above. However, because hypotheses can never be 100% verified, as they are capable of being disproved by contrary evidence or experiments, if we accept a hypothesis, it is not based on sure, solid fact. A belief is something we have which is not based on solid fact; as such, scientists have to work based upon belief. You have to believe certain hypotheses to develop others, and you act and live as though certain hypotheses are true even while admitting they might be false. This is faith or belief. To deny it involves a contradiction.

Arguably, each side has a point, although how far the debate rests on what 'hypothesis' means in science needs to be considered. In scientific usage the term 'hypothesis' is used in two ways: one as a theory to be tested, but also it means a very well-established set of observations and concepts about how the world works. However, if one wants to take an extremely sceptical stance (following the radical doubt of Descartes or the Zhuangzi), you could say that even well-established theories are not 100% certain. Whether that is a useful approach is debatable; however, my aim is to show each side what the other is talking about. As such, rather than each side simply shouting their position (i.e. 'science is *not* based on faith' or 'science *is* based on faith'), a more constructive disagreement could be had if each side explained how they are using the word faith and why they think it does or does not apply. Understanding your opponent's argument is always better than simply saying, 'You're wrong and have no valid opinions'. It is also the basis upon which you can start showing why they're wrong!

2

BOOKS AND BELIEFS
Choosing and Interpreting Texts

$\bigcirc \bigcirc \bigcirc$

THE HISTORY BIT

One common criticism of religions is that they are rigid and inflexible because they accept revealed truths found in books written hundreds or thousands of years ago – often by powerful (and now very dead) men. To some extent this is true; however, it also shows a clear misunderstanding of the way that religion, like any human institution, develops and evolves.

We begin by discussing what is called hermeneutics, which is the art of interpretation, or how books are read; indeed, interpretation/hermeneutics is not just about books as we constantly interpret all of our experience. We then discuss something about the way that collections of religious books, or scriptures, often termed the canon (meaning 'rule' or 'measure') in Christian usage, came together. We also discuss the nature of belief. This will also lead us to ask some questions about the way that humans (atheist, religious or of any persuasion) use books and sources of authority.

Interpreting the text

Hermeneutics, the art of interpretation, exists because scriptures are never simple. Like any other text, scriptures do not arrive with a clear set of meanings. While we will discuss violence in more detail in Chapter 5, one example is the way that Christians and Muslims (though they are not the only ones) read their respective scriptures either as teachings of peace and compassion, even pacifism, or justifications for war and violence. Again, many Christians see the teaching that Jesus is divine and the doctrine of the Trinity as embedded within the New Testament texts, while some Christians and scholars argue that neither of these presumptions are found there. Is one side right and the other wrong? That answer may be too simple, as we are dealing with human beings as 'interpreting' beings who bring a lot of ideas to any text; an example is given in the extended discussion of Gandhi in Box 2.1.

Box 2.1

Gandhi and the Bhagavad Gita

It is well known that one of Mohandas (Mahatma) Gandhi's (1869–1948) favourite texts was the Bhagavad Gita (c. second century BCE) from which he took his message of non-violence, or *ahimsa* (a better translation, though, may be 'non-harm'). However, the story is about a war between two rival family groups for control of a kingdom, and in it, Lord Krishna, an *avatar* (a being who has descended from the divine to human realm) of the Hindu deity Vishnu, reveals himself and explains that Arjuna, the principal character and a prince and warrior in one of the families, should not worry about fighting and killing his family and former friends. His reasoning is based on three main points:

- Arjuna is born as a warrior, and so it is his duty – in Sanskrit the term is *dharma*, which has various meanings but here refers to his position within society – to fight and kill.

- Because souls are eternal, he is not actually 'killing' anyone in any essential sense but merely destroying a particular body.

- By practising the yoga of devotion and action, Arjuna can perform his duty without hatred but merely as an outward action of his body, while his soul remains focused on Krishna and compassion. (Readers should be aware that this is a very different usage of yoga from the one with which they are probably familiar, which concerns physical postures and breathing techniques.)

At one level, the text's message is the absolute reverse of Gandhi's reading, but by seeking a message within it, Gandhi understood that it actually delivered a critique of violence and aggression, an interpretation which has been influential.

Obviously, we can't just say that any text can mean anything we want, but to read any text is always about negotiating meaning between the reader, the authorial intention and a community or society that provides concepts in which we come to the text. Gandhi's reading, for instance, was done in the context of several thousand years of tradition about non-violence in an Indian religious context. Muslims who understand the Qur'an as a teaching of peace read it through the fact that every verse attributes the words 'most merciful' to Allah as his key quality, and the very first chapter of the text emphasizes compassion and forgiveness as the attributes of this deity.

Indeed, when you come to the Qur'an, you will have read other books, talked to people about books and lived in a society that tells you certain things about what words mean, how an argument works and so forth. We therefore come to books as interpreting creatures in interpreting societies. Why is this important when we come to the hermeneutics of religious books? There are several answers, and one of them is the basic point that no text has one simple and obvious meaning (or, if it does, it is probably not a very good book). This is as true of religious scriptures as anything else. Another answer is that every religious community has, throughout history, developed methods and theories of interpretation – even to say you should understand a book literally is an act of interpretation about how the text should be read! A final answer to mention is that these methods of interpretation change and develop over time, which is well catalogued in the history of religions. No one book has been read in only one way by any religious community – and normally there are competing schools of interpretation at all times. Therefore, to say that religions are tied to old ways of understanding religious texts is simply to be unaware of the way that religions have always interpreted their texts in new contexts and ways.

In the Christian tradition, a theologian called Origen (185– 254 CE) was the first person to talk about the method of interpretation at length. He established a fourfold system of hermeneutics, which lasted for over 1000 years (described in Box 2.2) in which literal readings were less important and readings that sought a 'hidden' message in the text were more important. For 1000 years or more this is the way most Christians read scripture. Things changed as we came into the modern period, partly during the Reformation, as it involved Protestants rejecting much of the tradition that had built up over the centuries. Partly, this was about challenging the way the Bible was read and also how it was translated and made available to the common person. (For centuries it had only been in Latin, so only educated people, generally in ecclesiastical circles, had access.) While these events did not stop many allegorical meanings, it broke the power and influence of the scholastic monks of the Middle Ages and their established patterns of interpretation.

While some may argue that the reason why the Bible was restricted is because the patriarchal elite wanted to control the power, it was also the case that they thought both people and the text needed to be protected – a worry was that ignorant people might take the text and read it (or parts of it) literally and thereby misunderstand the wider implications and context, which was needed to truly understand it. However, it was particularly during the Enlightenment of the eighteenth century, when a historical and critical understanding arose, that a new attitude to the texts arose.

Box 2.2

Origen and Christian hermeneutics

The four methods of interpretation are the literal, ethical, allegorical and analogical. The literal was generally considered the lowest and least important, which was basically understanding the text as a historical narrative, so Jesus' miracle of Feeding the Five Thousand (Matthew 14.13–21) was considered to be a record of an event that had happened. However, it was also held that more or less every text in scripture could be read at other levels. These levels included the ethical, that is, what moral lesson could be learnt from it, and the allegorical, which was about using the text to gain either a spiritual insight or an insight into something else. However, the highest was the analogical level, which revealed knowledge about the end times (eschatology) when it was believed that Jesus would return in glory. Because of these levels of reading, most modern readers find medieval Christian exegesis (the act of interpreting a specific text) fairly obscure, as much of it used the religious imagination to create symbolic and analogical interpretations which can seem odd to us. Indeed, in Origen's commentary on the passage noted above he discusses whether the five fish equal our five senses and whether it was spiritual or earthly bread at length. Indeed, there was a saying that the more difficult the interpretation, the truer it was, indicating that only by poring over the text to produce difficult-to-find meanings could truth be reached.

There are two important trends in historical–critical study that come from the European Christian context. One of them came from scholars like Hermann Samuel Reimarus (1694–1768), who looked at the New Testament texts and realized that the portrayal of Jesus in church tradition – as the divine Son of God and second figure of the Trinity – did not match the more human figure in the Gospels. We should note that some Christians had realized this already in the Reformation when they came to the Bible, and so some Christian denominations, like the Quakers, had long disputed the divinity of Jesus. However, arguably more significant than any particular detail is the method, which was a questioning and critical approach that asked what history lay behind the text. It wasn't just atheists and freethinkers who adopted this, but it became during the nineteenth century a method for Christian theologians to read the Bible, although it was only accepted across all major denominations in the twentieth century. As such, reading the Bible became equivalent to asking questions about history: What was the story and context behind what was described? Indeed, for Christian scholars, reading the text now involves realizing that the texts do not simply record history but are already acts of interpretation by a community; somebody had made a choice of what to write down and was trying to tell his readers something (of course, it was a 'he'). It is noteworthy that often religious readings of texts (at least from academic theologians) are far more sophisticated than what we see amongst either fundamentalist believers or many atheist critics.

A different trend, however, but very closely related to the critical approach to seeing the text as history, was reading the text as a literal and infallible guide. Partially, this is a traditional way of reading it, and before the modern period, it didn't occur to most people to ask questions about the historical reliability of any authoritative text – as mentioned above, the symbolic readings mattered more, so it was realized that the literal truth could sometimes be presented in a way that pointed to something else; however, this way was also quite radically new, for instead of being of lesser importance than the message behind the text, believing in the literal meaning – and the literal meaning alone – became pretty much the assurance of a *correct* way of interpreting the text. Throughout Christian history, though, influential voices had previously stressed the significance of a literal approach, and Thomas Aquinas (1225–1274) was one such voice (although he was considered unorthodox in his day). For Aquinas, no ethical or symbolic reading could run counter to what appeared to be the literal and straightforward meaning of the text. Nevertheless, he still saw the higher meanings, following Origen, in going beyond the simple literal reading.

The focus on the literal alone is associated with what would be termed 'fundamentalism' in the USA or conservative evangelical in the UK (although some may like terms for themselves like 'Bible-believing Christians'). As such, the idea that the text should be read absolutely literally as a true and infallible history is in many ways quite a modern idea; indeed, in some ways it is simply a reversal or reaction against the historical–critical scholarly method (see Box 2.3). If the text is primarily a true account of history and relating facts, rather than symbols or the telling of ethical tales, then it demanded a new approach to every letter of that text as an exact fact. It is notable that we can draw one clear distinction between this modern approach, which Christians like to label 'traditional' today: it assumes that there is a clear and straightforward meaning to the text. This, we must note, differs from the actual tradition of interpretation which thought truth was only found in the most difficult or obscure reading of the text. Certainly, as we will discuss below, there are lots of problems with this novel approach to being Christian and reading Christian texts when we look from where the texts come.

Box 2.3

Reading the Bible literally: A modern concern?
Let's consider for a moment how radically different modern ways of reading the Bible – and modern *Christian* ways of reading the Bible (literalist or fundamentalist tendencies) – are from traditional concepts. Some people have claimed that fundamentalism as a phenomenon is essentially a modern one (a subject which is beyond the scope of our discussion). However, the idea that knowledge and ideas are primarily factual and conceptual is something which arose over the past few centuries in Western thought and dominates our modern ways of thinking and knowing. Can we imagine going to a book (assuming we don't see it as a work of fiction or fantasy) and thinking that whether it is factually true or not is not relevant to

us, but rather we are asking what are the symbolic truths it holds? We are not then reading the text in its surface meaning (e.g. whether it tells us the sky is blue, whether Rome has 50,000 inhabitants, whether someone slept or was awake) but always reading *behind* the text and asking what message this conveys. Even with a work of fiction, we are reading the story, and even if we don't think it's true, we accept the world it presents to us. Even if we think there is a moral to the story, we get there *through* the story. In a pre-modern reading we are continually asking what every word in the account means in order to find a deeper message. It is more like looking at a work of art than what most contemporary people would see as 'reading a book'. We are talking about pre-modern art (but some more recent art too), where there was a world of symbols to be read; for example, the colours each had their own significance and the background images were not simply to look pretty but rather were symbols meant to impart information to the knowledgeable reader or viewer. In this light it can be seen why, despite claims to represent 'tradition', modern Christian conservatives, fundamentalists or literalists (however they are termed) are not actually traditional but rather represent a very modern approach to the text which reads the surface as the true meaning and looks for facts and knowledge in the literal, rather than the symbolic, layers.

Collecting the canon

Our next question is: Who collected the books? As we have mentioned, the term 'canon' became used in Christianity to describe the texts that became its scripture. However, these books did not suddenly materialize from the sky one day but were written by human beings as part of their developing communities. The Christian Bible is composed of two sets of books, the Old Testament (or Hebrew Bible) and the New Testament; however, it is not a simple or clear question as to which books should be in either of them or why they're there, although we should not overstress the mystery behind the collection.

The Old Testament is a Christian term for the texts they inherited from Judaism. Scholars and theologians these days tend to use the term Hebrew Bible, as the Christian terminology is obviously derogatory to Jews – because the *Old* Testament is superseded by the *New* Testament. (Some theologians suggest using First and Second Testament, which overcomes the theological sense of what is termed 'supersessionism', whereby one religion is made obsolete, or is overridden, by another.) Now this may seem straightforward because Christians claim they simply took over the books used in Judaism; however, it is not that straightforward. In Jesus' time there was no single set of texts used by all Jews; indeed, what was probably the most commonly used set of texts was a Greek-language version called the Septuagint (from the Greek word for seventy, believed to be the number of scholars who did the translation).

The Septuagint, however, contained texts written originally in Greek and were probably largely unknown to many Jews in the Palestine of Jesus' day; nevertheless, they were used by Jews who lived elsewhere – probably the majority of Jews at that time. Because Christianity spread around the Roman Empire, it was the wider community and their texts, which they understood to be the Jewish scriptures. As such, early Christianity took over the Hebrew Bible as found in the Septuagint. However, following the destruction of the Temple in Jerusalem by the Romans (70 CE), what would become Rabbinic Judaism (what we call Judaism today) started to formulate its own identity, and this involved determining what texts it used. Legend tells us this was determined in a single meeting; however, it was far more likely a process – especially as it would take time to spread and become mainstream Judaism. This decision limited the books only to those believed to have originally been written in Hebrew; therefore, a specific Jewish canon was formulated, which differed from what the Christians used. As Christians, at least in the West, used a Latin translation and (at that time) saw no value in studying Hebrew, this fact did not come to light until the Renaissance when the study of classical languages, including Hebrew, was revived; but it was the Reformation that saw it become a major issue.

Reformers like Martin Luther (1483–1546) sought to distance themselves from the Roman Catholic Church, which they argued had created new traditions to add onto the beliefs of the earliest church, so this discrepancy in the Hebrew Bible became important. Not knowing the historical circumstances which had led to Christians adopting their Old Testament, the reformers claimed that Roman Catholics had added new books to it and limited their own use of texts to what was then used by Jews. This had a practical use as well: Protestants rejected prayer for the dead, and the most clear biblical injunction for this was included in one of the texts they rejected (2 Maccabees). This history is important, because it illustrates the way that scripture is not simply the basis of tradition, but rather is a two-way process of a tradition choosing at a specific time what books it would include. Later, this canon may have seemed a normative or irrefutable revelation, but it was not always so; however, for Christianity, the New Testament texts are the most significant.

Like the Old Testament, the New Testament has a history. At first, as a Jewish sect, the early Jesus Movement had no texts of its own but simply used Jewish scriptures; however, in due course, texts came to be written. The first of these texts were the letters of Paul and also those of a number of other early Christian leaders. Later, as the first generation of Jesus' disciples were dying out, to preserve their memory, the Gospels – the term simply means 'good news' or 'glad tidings' – were written, and they were records of Jesus' life and sayings. A number of other texts were added as time went on. At first there was no attempt to collect or systematize these, but around the middle of the second century CE a Christian leader called Marcion (85–160 CE) collected the first Christian canon which contained an edited version of Luke's Gospel and various of Paul's letters amongst other works. In response, rival Christian leaders made their own collections, and the first collection of Christian texts were then basically an attempt to claim a 'true' lineage back to Jesus and his disciples by having the texts which showed that *your* teachings were in these texts. To somewhat circumvent our story, one particular lineage won out, what became mainstream Catholic and Orthodox (and therefore, over 1000 years later, Protestant) Christianity, and with remarkable success it made its books *the* Christian tradition, such that until the nineteenth century the books it used were really the only New Testament that anyone knew.

Several things need to be emphasized here. First, this victory meant that other Christian traditions were branded as heretical, so most standard histories of Christianity will tell you that Marcion was a Gnostic, one brand of heretic, and that he created a 'Gnostic Bible'. However, in the earliest Christian centuries these categories simply did not exist – but the winners got to name, and therefore sideline, the losers. As such, conventional church history paints it as a single true tradition defending itself against aberrant innovations attacking it on all sides, with brave defenders upholding a lineage from Jesus and his disciples to the church as it exists today. It is now very hard for us to know who, if anyone, best represented a 'true' lineage (if such a thing exists) as basically every side claimed this, but the winners destroyed many of the texts of those who lost; therefore, many of the different traditions of early Christianity are generally unknown to us. What we do know, however, is that many of those branded as heretics were at various times more numerous than the later orthodox group and also included many of what would seem to be the most respected and pretty much mainstream leaders of Christian communities in their own day, such as Valentinus (second century CE), who was an influential leader in the church in Rome.

Second, what became the victorious side in collecting its texts used a specific criteria for inclusion in what became its canon, which was that the texts were either written by those directly connected to Jesus' disciples or very close to the early disciples. Indeed, given the limitations of their resources to assess this, it has to be said that they did a pretty good job. The four Gospels they included are probably the earliest ones and very likely go back to sources near, or not too far removed from, Jesus' disciples (we address some others in Box 2.4). The set of Paul's letters contain primarily those which almost certainly were written by Paul – others claiming to be by Paul existed but were rejected – although scholars are pretty certain a few in the canon are not genuinely by Paul, while others are suspect. Of course, Paul did not know Jesus during his life but has generally been considered amongst the disciples by the Christian community. Along with Acts, probably written by the author of Luke's Gospel, this makes up the vast majority of the New Testament as being as close as we can get to early sources. (Of course, one thing we don't know is whether other early letters by disciples were destroyed or lost over the years, because it didn't fit the agenda of the winners – although we cannot argue from lack of evidence to support conspiracy theories.) Most of the Gospels that were rejected were written from the second century CE onwards and so are considerably later, while other letters and various texts claiming to be the Acts of particular apostles (i.e. the Acts of Peter) are likewise later sources. One significant text, though, is the Gospel of Thomas, which many scholars believe contains very early source material and probably genuine sayings of Jesus, which either parallel ones in the four biblical Gospels or are entirely new and independent stories; however, as we have it, it contains what appear to be some second-century material as well.

Box 2.4

Lost Gospels

Archaeology has dramatically changed our understanding of early Christian texts and traditions, and one important aspect of this has been the discovery of many new Gospels. These texts are generally labelled Gnostic, which is a loose and often confusing term but has some coherent use in this context. In general, these texts represent Jesus as a divine manifestation and are far divorced from narratives of his earthly life as represented in the more familiar Gospels, especially those of Matthew, Mark and Luke. It is quite correct that these were suppressed and often destroyed or marginalized by what became the mainstream church. However, they are not lost sources in our knowledge of Jesus – except as discussed in the Gospel of Thomas. Not a single one dates from the first century, and they are much later texts, often written by groups with little link to the historical figure of Jesus. As such, they are important sources for looking at how Christianity was developing in the second and third centuries particularly, but not for looking back to the first century or the life of Jesus (which we discuss further in Chapter 3).

Third, we also know that the New Testament material, as it stands, is far from consistent, and the version used for around 2000 years by Christians contains numerous differences from the very earliest manuscript versions that archaeology has discovered.

In summary, in assessing the reliability of the Christian Bible as a text, we have something of a mixed bag. For those looking to support the mainstream Christian tradition there is good evidence that it contains early sources and texts, which on the whole equate to the texts inherited from Judaism and those that come in a lineage that descends as close as possible to sources near to Jesus' disciples. Particularly for the New Testament we have a set of texts generally reliably collected with a clear rationale and, it is noted, were used by what became mainstream traditions in more or less the number we now have, 27, from around the late second century. This set of 27 seems well established in the subsequent century, even if an official statement waited until the fourth century. However, against this position, we know that mistakes were made, especially in relation to a few of Paul's letters, and, moreover, that the texts were edited and altered over the course of several centuries, so any claim to absolute certainty about the texts' reliability is simply historically impossible. It is a parody of the truth, though, to see the texts as solely the product of later centuries; we are dealing with mainly first-century texts, with archaeology and textual analysis revealing only 'tampering' – not wholesale rewriting on the vast majority. We also know that texts important to many early Christians, including what are as close to being genuine sayings of Jesus as anything in the Bible, were not included, while some may be lost. Before saying any more about what this means for interpretation, I will address a final point: additional books.

As we have seen, scripture never simply appeared but was made. Even the idea that certain books could or should be seen as scripture came from internal disputes and claims to authority by rival factions. We can even put it this strongly: the Bible came not from divine revelation but was made by certain groups seeking to enforce their interpretation (notwithstanding that many of the individual writers no doubt wrote with a sense of spiritual conviction and even a sense of speaking from God). Indeed, a fixed and determined canon only came with a political victory by one party. Nevertheless, this never stopped people adding books. While the mainstream Christian canon was closed from about the fourth century CE, Christians were also writing new texts to explain how the others should be read, and which often became more important. For many Protestants, Luther's works and ideas are the chief key to interpreting scripture (they would not put it like this, but they read scripture through that lens), while many will look to figures like Benedict of Nursia (c. 480–547) or Ignatius of Loyola (1491–1556) for a guide on how to live a Christian life. As we said, it is all about interpretation and so whatever books are accepted as scripture are always read in the light of a community which often includes other books. Perhaps the most important 'texts', though, are what came to be called the Creeds. While not books, Christians came to accept the definition of their belief to be summed up in written statements of faith made by major councils. Most important of these is what is termed the Nicene Creed (325/451 CE) – the term 'creed' itself comes from the Greek words they begin with which means 'we believe' (though often translated as 'I believe') – which Catholic, Orthodox and Protestant Christians see as the central statement of Christian belief. (We will discuss some aspects of this further when we discuss Jesus in the next chapter and who he may have been.) Importantly, for over 1500 years some of the most influential Christians in the world, and therefore influential interpreters of Christianity, have read the Bible through the lens of this communal statement of faith.

Revelation, interpretation and significant books

As stated earlier, everything comes down to interpretation, but it may be suggested that some ways of interpreting texts are better than others. Today, anyone who wishes to maintain a literal interpretation of the Bible as the true word of God must do so in ignorance of the actual nature of that text, or of the actual collection of those texts. Indeed, to claim that such a reading is true to the texts is also very problematic. As we have noted, the texts that form the New Testament were collected on the grounds that they were the closest witnesses to Jesus and his disciples – not that they were 'supernatural revelation' sent down from God. Indeed, two factors mitigate against this: One is the internal evidence of the texts themselves. For instance, Acts begins by stating that the material in it can be testified to by witnesses; if it had been given by God as revealed truth, what need would there have been for this? The second factor is that one reason for rejecting many of the later Gospels and other texts for inclusion is that they claimed to be 'revelation', that is, material revealed in divine dreams or by supernatural means. Instead, the compilers wanted to show clear human writers who could be named and shown in lineages traced back by the community. Books were included because they were believed to be human products, not supernatural products! Of course, over the centuries this was forgotten and so the canon of scripture gained a sense of supernatural truth or revelation, while it was generally held that the authors were reliable witnesses. I would suggest, though, that today these books need to be approached in a very different way.

While I have focused on the Christian scriptures, we could look at the historical collection of any set of scriptural texts from any religious tradition or even from non-religious texts. However, it would take too long to discuss the complexities of every tradition here. In principle, though, a similar system takes place in that a community of interpretation reads the texts in different ways to suit their needs, and it is also the community which decides which texts get included. Importantly, the authority given to the text tends to become more fixed through time as it changes from being understood as a collection of the community into being a sacred text. Some communities, though, create sacred texts from the very beginning, and Islam is a case in point. The Qur'an is believed to be a collection of utterances of the Prophet Muhammad made under divine inspiration from God. As such, it is distinguished from the *hadith*, which is the collection of his sayings, and while these are important as the words of Muhammad, they are not words from God. (As an important note, the term 'Allah' is simply the Arabic term for '[the] God', not a name for the Islamic deity; as such, it makes sense to say 'God' in English when speaking about Islam's deity. Arabic-speaking Jews and Christians call their God 'Allah'; indeed, all three traditions believe that their deity is the God of Abraham and so often understand that they are talking about the same deity.) It is also noted that the idea of interpretation does not just apply to religious texts, as all texts need interpretation. Any student of law or constitution will realize this, as the laws of the land or a constitutional text are not simply read so people know what it says. Rather, they are interpreted and argued over; hence, we see the whole field of constitutional law, which exists to interpret and understand these texts in the context of the evolving societies in which they exist. Indeed, the understanding of them also evolves over time. (While we do not have the space to go into this here, the way that religion and the state, for instance, are understood to relate in countries like the USA, Singapore or India change over time.)

It is also noteworthy that seeing specific texts or sources as influential or important is not simply a religious trait, or something found in those traditions we call religious. As discussed in Chapter 1, it is hard to identify any specific traits that clearly separate all those things we call 'religions' from those things we don't call religions. Marxism is a case in point, and many will look to the texts of Marx or Engels as founding narratives, even suggesting that they provide a truth that can't be questioned. Likewise, specific texts may be foundational for many in philosophical schools, whether they are interested in existential philosophy, for instance, and may find books by Jean-Paul Sartre (1905–1980) inspirational for how they live their lives.

As with religious texts, philosophical or even scientific texts are also interpreted by their readers and find their meaning and significance within this context. Some, for instance, will read Charles Darwin's (1809–1882) *Origin of the Species* (1859) as a foundational part of an atheist world view (a matter we will discuss further in Chapter 7). However, it is noted that Darwin himself lost his Christian faith for more personal reasons, while many other scientists in his day, and since then, do not find this text nor evolution a threat to their religious belief. As such, the meaning we take from texts varies, as does their significance for our lives and beliefs.

Another important factor to consider is the way that human beings tend to place great reliance upon texts, especially those they consider to have authority. Speaking from personal experience, I have had atheists tell me, against presentation of facts to the contrary, that they know something is true because they read it in one of Dawkins' books. Like a religious scripture, it is treated as an inerrant, (i.e. infallible) authority! I don't think it is useful to respond by saying there are both stupid atheists and stupid religious people. Also, intelligent people put great weight on selected books. Rather, we need to think about the way that written works are perceived to carry great weight. Today, of course, for many people the Internet works in a similar way. I am sure all of us have had someone, even intelligent people, tell us that something is true because they read it online. Of course, nobody claims that Dawkins or Darwin have supernatural origins, and so their works are not identical to attitudes to certain scriptural texts, but it is, first, too simplistic to simply say that all religious texts are considered to have supernatural origins either, and second, wrong to say that this means they are treated and interpreted differently.

THINKING ABOUT SACRED TEXTS TODAY

Thinking about the way that human beings tend to treat written sources of authority we can ask: What should we make of religious texts today? We know that all religious texts have a history that has led to some being accepted and others rejected, while they have been changed and edited over the years – this, of course, does not just apply to Christian texts but to Buddhist texts and those of every religious tradition. It is also clear that the interpretation of such texts is never simply about reading the texts themselves. For Christians, of course, there may be a feeling that these texts link them into a community history and need to be considered and interpreted again today. For atheists, no such responsibility exists, so does this mean that they should simply ignore the scriptures of the world's religions? Why listen to the words of someone who lived hundreds or even thousands of years ago whose world view and beliefs may have been entirely antithetical and irrelevant to one's own? Indeed, some atheists will make these claims: Why listen to Bronze Age or Iron Age ethics or world views that are not relevant now?

If we stop for a minute, we may note that people don't tend to say this about Shakespeare's plays, Sunzi's *Art of War*, Plato's philosophy, Rumi's poetry or Aristophanes' plays. Just because these people lived long ago in very different times with very different beliefs, we still think that we can enjoy the texts as story, as narratives of human adventure or as attempts to ask big questions about the human situation and our place in it. Is the Bible, the Dhammapada, the Ramayana or the Qur'an any different? Many religious believers may, of course, say that they are – they are revelation or inspired in some way – but for someone without this baggage they still form part of the world's literary and cultural heritage. Perhaps, even, they have truths from which people can learn? Certainly, for Christians or other believers who take on board the historical critical enquiry of the past few hundred years, the approach to these texts will be very different from that of our ancestors, or even from that of more fundamentalist Christians living today. How do you make sense of scripture that is flawed, changed and possibly even included in the canon by mistake? Reflecting on these questions is important for anyone coming to spirituality in today's world.

Let's start with some ground rules and see where this takes us. If we assume that many of the great religious figures of world history, like Jesus (c. 4 BCE–30 CE), the Buddha, Guru Nanak (1469–1539), Gandhi (1869–1948) or Martin Luther King Jr (1929–1968) were capable of inspiring others, speaking out against injustice or simply good at guiding people to live meaningful and fulfilled lives, then it may be worth looking at their ideas. Obviously, this doesn't mean that we have to believe everything they said or were reported to have said – we know the Christian books certainly do not tell us exactly what Jesus said (but we *are* on firmer ground with Martin Luther King Jr) – but their general message may nevertheless hold truths from which we can learn. Jesus' recommendation to be as a young child could be seen as a very psychologically healthy direction, that is, to be prepared to see wonder in the world around us and accept life without pre-judgements and suspicions (although obviously not naively, and Jesus was certainly ready to challenge and call out those he thought were misleading others). Our first ground rule, then, is to assume that the world's great spiritual leaders may have a message we can learn from *today*.

As a further point on this, returning to something noted above, today people will read texts like Shakespeare, or maybe Homer's *Iliad*, as inspiring to themselves. It is not simply that we can look back to the religious texts of the past to provide relevance today, but we could read *A Thousand and One Nights*, Li Bai's poetry, Sappho's poetry or the writings of Cicero. If we can look to these works, then why not also to those texts we traditionally label religious – especially as many of these artistic works, while often seen as 'secular' by us, have religious underpinnings or contexts?

A second point is that the interpretation we make of the texts or messages is whatever is relevant and meaningful to us today. As we discussed, throughout history people have interpreted their scriptures in new ways according to the times, and so this approach, far from being innovative or new, is actually 'traditional'. The theologian Paul Tillich (1886–1965) developed a method he called the 'Theology of Correlation', which meant finding out how the Christian message could be applied to today's contemporary situation, but as he pointed out, this was not a new method he'd thought of, but was what had been done down the centuries. If a message is not put in terms people can understand and related to their context, then it simply won't be understood or be comprehensible. Therefore, the onus is not to understand things in traditional ways, but in contemporary ways, which is our second rule.

The second rule, to be contemporary, needs to be tempered by a third, which is to pay attention to tradition. How do we know who we are? From where we have come? What ideas mean? The answer, almost always, is to pay attention to where things have come from and recognize that we are part of a community, a tradition: our ideas and thoughts are shaped by those around us, and so to some degree, at least, by those who came before us. Indeed, I would say this is essential. Why do we know that we should not take scripture literally and as inerrant truth? The answer is simply by paying attention to the past. If those who wrote the New Testament saw themselves simply as human recorders of other people who had known a remarkable person (although of course putting their own interpretation and context into what they recorded), then we must likewise understand their writings in this way. However, we also need to understand something about what those texts meant to those who wrote them, and about the community which interprets them, if we are to make any sense of them. If we return to Gandhi, his understanding of the Bhagavad Gita as a text leading us to non-violence did not simply materialize out of nowhere, but rather from a tradition and community that valued these principles. Of course, there are always competing interpretations and competing traditions, so we may ask what we should make of them.

To answer the question we have just asked, we need to invoke a fourth rule, which many express as human flourishing, to do good unto others or, put simply into one word: ethics. It may well be that we do not need books, texts, scriptures or religion to do good to other people and treat them well – indeed, religions have, at times, taught us the opposite – but does that mean that we can do without them? Perhaps we can, and certainly one can be a just and humane atheist or humanist, and I would suggest that the Enlightenment legacy that fought against religious discrimination is vital to the world we now have. However, the fight against slavery was led by evangelical Christians who believed that all people were essentially equal and so should be treated as such. Indeed, religious traditions provide a fountain of positive endorsements to moral and ethical behaviour that underlie much contemporary thinking, and certainly foreshadow much that happened in the Enlightenment. (This is not to say it is all good, and every religion has a legacy of violence and unjust behaviour; see Chapter 5). Indeed, ethical questions are not always straightforward, but are often complex and may involve us needing to balance and weigh the rights and duties we owe to one person against those we owe to another – the philosopher Jacques Derrida (1930–2004) suggests that ethics are always flawed, because the duty I owe to one person must always conflict with the duty I owe to another. Centuries of ethical debates on such questions have been argued by religious thinkers and philosophers, and while we may not always agree with them, it seems presumptuous to say that we can learn nothing from the deliberations of many of the most educated women and men (who were sometimes excluded; see Chapter 6) whose intellect and moral insights led others to keep and value their thoughts. For instance, in Catholic moral thought, a principle, largely developed by their great medieval thinker Thomas Aquinas, is the law of double effect, which determines that one should look to the intention of an act if a potential harm may result. To give a classic example, a woman is pregnant but falls fatally ill, and the only possible cure will result in the death of her child. What to do? How do we weigh the saving of one life with the taking of another (assuming here that one sees, as Aquinas and others did and do, the unborn baby as a person)? The law of double effect argues that to cure the mother is legitimate, because the aim is not to kill the unborn child but to save the mother. Given that doing nothing would result in two deaths, it becomes legitimate not to take one life to save another, but to enact a cure which has the unintended (even if inevitable) consequence of taking the potential life. But this, nevertheless, prevents a greater harm: two deaths. One need not be pro- or anti-abortion, or even Catholic, to see that a potentially useful principle for thinking about moral decisions is found here. Similar examples could, of course, be taken from other religious traditions and also from secular sources, but religion should not be ignored in thinking about such questions.

Of course, there are a number of tricky questions I have not elaborated on here. Those who see themselves as equally committed to human flourishing and doing good have quite radically opposed moral beliefs, and much that we think of as our basic ethical attitude is imprinted upon us by our culture so that it can seem quite natural to us. Animal rights, abortion, capitalism and many other things are all issues on which very rational, caring and just people can find themselves deeply divided. However, such divisions occur as much amongst people of one religion as amongst agnostics, atheists and others. It is not my intention here to suggest what I see as an answer to various moral questions – that would be another book and another context – although many indications, which I hope would be conducive or persuasive to the reader, as to my opinions in various areas will no doubt arise. Settling such issues is something that simply cannot be done here; however, the question of ethics is always present in this book and is addressed more closely in Chapter 8.

It may strike the reader that in a chapter entitled 'Books and Beliefs' remarkably little has been said about any specific beliefs. We have seen that Christians are on the whole united around things like the Nicene Creed (notwithstanding that for several centuries it was a minority position amongst all Christians globally and that historical happenchance has made it more or less normative today) but have not said much about what they are. This is very much intentional as this chapter has primarily focused on issues about where beliefs come from and what significance we should attach to them if we focus on religious texts. To the orthodox, committed Christian the critical question may be: Where is the outline of those key central beliefs? However, as may be guessed, I tend to deem beliefs as somewhat historically derived artefacts. Of course, we all have beliefs; I have beliefs about the nature of reality, the best route to get to the supermarket, who the world's best tennis player is and many others. As human beings we are creatures that create meaning and systems of belief that help us navigate the world around us; however, I do not believe that we can prescribe correct beliefs. This is not to say that I would endorse an 'anything goes' approach and would rigorously oppose anyone who believed that causing harm to animals for pleasure was good, or that racism was justified. Indeed, I would also contend that some religious beliefs are in some ways 'better' or more credible or beneficial than others. However, I also hold that people do immensely good acts out of beliefs I could not entertain: to take a recent example, many of the medical staff who went to West Africa in response to the Ebola outbreak in 2014 were inspired to do so by an evangelical Christian faith.

As we proceed, we will certainly address questions of belief, and indeed this chapter has no doubt assaulted what many people would see as their core religious beliefs. As stated, some beliefs are more credible than others. If I state the truth as I see it, it will inevitably conflict with what other people see to be truth. Certainly many atheist spokespeople and religious apologists often are quite combative in their language, but I am not aiming to convert anyone from one side to another. Rather, my aim is simply to look at areas where there is misunderstanding and disagreement, and this may come from either camp. I hope what is offered will be useful to both discuss these areas more deeply and appreciate the other's point of view. At the same time, I will suggest what I think we should make of the evidence, which may sometimes be uncomfortable to both sides, but I am not here to set out new beliefs or suggest some way that people should reconcile atheism and religious belief. Therefore, rather than arguing which path we should accept, this chapter has looked at the nature of books and the way that people understand and use them.

In the next chapter, we will consider some figures, such as Jesus, the Buddha and Muhammad, often discussed in those scriptural books.

3

AUTHORITY FIGURES
Jesus and the Others

O O O

THE HISTORY BIT

The world's religions have often been in conflict over the relationship of their various founding figures. Meanwhile, these figures have often been criticized in various ways by atheists. Some have founders who are clearly historically identifiable; the strident denial of Jesus and the Buddha has no academic credibility (see Box 3.1). Religions, or traditions, like Buddhism, Christianity, Islam, Confucianism and Sikhism look to their founders, or foundational figures, as significant. Other religions often have less easily identifiable historical figures, although certain figures are often looked to: Judaism looks to Moses (c. 1500 BCE?) and Abraham (c. 2000 BCE?) as significant patriarchs, although we can say nothing with any certainty about them. Daoism (also spelt Taoism) has the mythical Laozi (often spelt Lao Tze or Lao Tzu) envisaged as an elderly contemporary of Confucius (c. 551–479 BCE); however, his first biographer, Sima Qian (c. 145–87 BCE), recorded several stories of figures who he thought it might be but confessed he didn't know which, if any, was the alleged writer of the classic Daodejing (often spelt Tao Te Ching), and subsequent legends simply took the first one (however, there is no mythical sage who was the author of that text as we have it now). The Hindu family of religions also looks back to various figures, many to Krishna, narrated in the Bhagavad Gita or in other texts, but it is impossible to find any kind of historical basis for that story, although later founding figures of some Hindu traditions, like Swaminarayan (1781–1830), founder of the eponymous sect, are more clearly historical. In short, it may be asked what to make of the competing claims of the various founders made by their devotees.

Box 3.1

The historical or mythical Jesus?

While the vast majority of historians accept that Jesus was a historical figure, there have been many – what are often termed 'mythicists' – who insist he never existed. While the view has next to no academic credibility, it has a wide popular following and some seemingly credible spokespersons: Christopher Hitchens (1949–2011); Richard Carrier who has a related PhD; and Richard Price, a former professor. However, none of the arguments of these figures carries much credibility: Hitchens repeats basic misunderstandings about historical texts; Carrier employs a method not used by academic historians; and, before becoming an atheist and mythicist, Price was an evangelical professor at a conservative Christian university that never accepted scholarship on Jesus. Here are several of the main misconceptions on which the mythicist arguments are based:

- There are discrepancies in the stories (i.e. the Gospels), which suggest none of it is reliable.

- The stories relate miracles, which make them suspect.

- Elements of the stories show parallels with other older stories.

- The texts were written by advocates.

- Many other deity-type figures are mythical (i.e. Zeus, Ra and so forth), so Jesus probably is also.

Many of these points are discussed elsewhere in this chapter, as it is part of the 'bread and butter' of historians using historical and ancient source material; for instance, all notable figures of the ancient world performed miracles, but nobody thinks this means the life narratives of the Roman emperor Augustus are entirely fictitious because of this. Again, anyone who has dealt with witness testimony in court knows that finding identical accounts of something that even happened last week is both rare and suspicious. There are also good reasons to postulate that the Gospels give credible narratives.

For instance, increased knowledge of the period, coming partly from recent archaeological evidence, shows Jesus' teachings fit into the context of a first-century Galilean rabbi. It is worth addressing Carrier, who advances an argument using Bayes' theorem to help make his arguments seem scientific. This theorem relies on assessing probability based on directly comparable examples; however, as any historian will point out, any event or figure in history tends to be extremely contextual, that is, you cannot simply take a few surface similarities and decide to use them. When I came across someone seeking to advance the theorem within an academic context, it was thoroughly taken apart but not by biblical scholars or religious believers, but rather atheist ancient historians and textual scholars. Importantly, if the mythicists are right it means academic and professional historians and classical scholars don't know how to do their jobs, while literally tens of thousands of scholars (including many atheists) are covering up evidence that Jesus never existed. Given that, the prominent atheist Michael Ruse notes:

> There is a highly vocal group of deniers of the existence of Jesus. But frankly, they come across like most conspiracy theorists, overly passionate in their cause, unwilling to compromise, and (a sure sign) very touchy when you question their credentials.

The lives of Jesus and the Buddha

We will focus here on two of the founding figures, Jesus (c. 4 BCE–30 CE) and the Buddha (c. fifth century BCE). Comparison between these two figures has a long history in the encounter between the traditions, and various ways have been made to relate each to the other. To start, we see a number of clear similarities in the way they are portrayed: each is given a royal heritage in their 'biographies' (I put this in inverted commas because none of the life stories are biographies in any modern sense, on which I will say more); both are seen to stand as clear founders of a new tradition, though whether this is an accurate assessment of what they wanted to do is another question; both gather disciples and form a community, which in each case has (acquired) a male bias (see Chapter 6); and, finally, each is seen to have various miracles associated with them often seen as proof of their teachings or status. However, there are also numerous differences – arguably far more than the characteristics they share, and I won't list them, as any list tends to reflect a certain agenda depending on what someone wants to prove. For instance, many Christian apologists stress Jesus' humble life (notwithstanding the royal claims made for his lineage) compared with the splendour and wealth which was seen to surround the young Buddha, as well as what is seen as Jesus' self-sacrificial death, and indeed what are likewise seen as his claims to divinity, which is contrasted with the fact that the Buddha is seen as having been simply human. Nevertheless, as indicated, each of these points has a purpose and the claims are far from clear or straightforward, so we'll say something about each figure. (This will draw from the broad scholarly consensus, although some different interpretations exist on various matters.)

Jesus was probably born somewhere around 4 BCE in Nazareth, a very poor town in the Roman Province of Palestine, where he grew up as some kind of artisan. (The Greek term often translated as 'carpenter' is not precise.) Presumably, though, he was possessed of some exceptional intelligence and charisma, because he became a Rabbi, a teacher, in the style of those from Galilee – not as exacting about the precise prescriptions of the Jewish Law as those in Jerusalem, and probably with a strong regard for the oppressed masses of the countryside. It is very notable that most of his teaching occurs in provincial towns or in the countryside, and the great city of Sepphoris, which dominated the land around Nazareth is not mentioned at all; its very absence and the absence of other cities, apart from Jerusalem, is striking. He taught about the Kingdom of God, although his precise meaning is unclear (it may have been a future eschatological state or a present potential, or both), but he also taught in parables, often clear simple messages that would appeal to his listeners who were generally poorly educated and from the countryside (though some are presented as obscure). It is not clear how many times he visited Jerusalem, but one dramatic visit would be his last. That he was crucified shows that the Romans regarded him as a political threat, but not a serious one as his disciples were not all rounded up and also killed, which fits well with what we know of him and the Roman treatment of dissidents. That political ramifications surrounding his entry into Jerusalem seems clear, but if the event recorded in the Gospels of him riding an ass and having palm leaves laid before him occurred, it was not the grand entry into the city that is made out but would have been a small and fairly secretive affair, or else he would have been arrested and killed by the Romans without hesitation. As such, it was probably his overturning of the money changers' tables, which fits in with a number of scholarly views of him as a temple restoration prophet, that prompted his arrest and execution: the city was full of pilgrims, and the Romans were present in force to ensure no trouble occurred. The details of his trial before the Jewish authorities is rather odd as the Gospel accounts say they didn't have the authority to kill Jesus, which, if he was tried on religious grounds, they did. Those who know the biblical text will recall that one of Jesus' followers, Stephen, was stoned for his beliefs. This indicates that the charges against Jesus were entirely political; if he had been charged with heresy of some form the Jewish authorities could and would have stoned him. It will be clear that most of what I have said has covered Jesus' death and resurrection more than his life and teaching – a pattern which reflects the Gospels generally – however, in terms of Jesus' own teaching and career, this is probably secondary. It is the later tradition of his followers that comes to attach such importance to his final days, and evidence exists that a number of Jesus' followers found the teachings of primary significance. It would distract us too much here to recount in detail how his death became religiously charged and even has been seen as his primary work – indeed, as redemptive of all humanity. But notably, while the words attributed to Jesus – *Eloi, Eloi, la'ma sabachtha'ni?* ('My God, My God, why have You forsaken me?') (Mark 15.34) – may indicate that he died in despair believing his teachings and prophetic mission had failed, we know that his early followers soon became infused with hope and began preaching. The scholar Marcus Borg suggests that we need to look at two attitudes towards, and understandings of, Jesus: the first is the pre-Easter Jesus, when he was simply a rabbi/teacher whom they followed; the second is the post-Easter Jesus, when he was understood to have some form of transcendent role or significance. Perhaps, or quite likely, the disciples thought of Jesus pre-Easter as at least a potential prophet, or maybe even the Messiah, but this term, we should be aware, in the Jewish context is a person specially chosen by God to help usher in the Last Days, and it certainly would not have referred to any kind of divine figure.

Turning to the Buddha, whose name we are told was Siddhartha Gautama, we have far fewer historical certainties. At a minimum, all that we can really say is that he was born, became a renouncer – a wandering holy man – had an experience that he and others found of significance, taught and died. Nevertheless, some scholars suggest we can have historical certainty about a lot more material, and certainly there are aspects of his life story that are coherent and tenable enough that we can assume they are based on some historical facts. For instance, his father, in the legend, is seen as being a great emperor who was so powerful that he could protect his son from the sight of suffering and pain, and provided him with a palace for each season. However, it is clear that no such ruler could have existed; nevertheless, it is possible that his father was a tribal chieftain amongst a primarily agricultural people who would have regarded themselves as warrior stock and therefore of high social standing. There is a stray detail in his life narratives where he enters a trance when young, watching his father ploughing; in the story, a symbolic act when the ruler breaks the ground at the beginning of the farming season is credible. We are even given the names of his first two meditation teachers, and quite likely he practised and rejected the current schools and also practised extreme asceticism, which was advocated by some teachers of his day. After his awakening (in English the term 'enlightenment' is often used, but 'awakening' is a better translation), he went out and taught for about 50 years and gathered a community of monks, nuns and lay people. The stories of schisms in his community, the *sangha*, are probably reliable, as it is not a detail that a flattering disciple would make up.

He died from food poisoning due to a meal given by a follower, probably pork, as his monastic community initially accepted any food offered as an act of hospitality, but it is likely that vegetarianism was endorsed as an ideal from an early stage. Even today, many monks will accept non-vegetarian food when offered. Again, I have not said much about the Buddha's teachings, but it is likely that what we now know as the Four Noble Truths and Interdependent Origination all go back to the Buddha, as these relate very clearly to what seem to be his basic insights, while he taught a specific form of meditation focused on what we may term mindfulness, a term often used in Buddhist thought.

However, it is far from clear how systematic the Buddha's teachings were, and we cannot with certainly say that any words in the Buddhist scriptures are actually his.

Certainly, the record we have of each of these teachers lives has many dissimilarities, but both are fitted into similar patterns of religious figures before them. We have generally left out what are seen as the more miraculous elements of the stories, but special births, signs and portents attend their lives. It is far from an indication, though, that the life story of each is nothing but an amalgam of previous religious myths to 'create' a new religious leader, as some critics have claimed. Rather, such elements are simply part of the human pattern of storytelling: we make sense of any story by fitting it into the narratives we already have. It is also the way that people would have made sense of these ideas in that context: if other religious figures have remarkable births, you give yours a remarkable birth too so that readers know the sort of character. This does, however, mean that it becomes harder to distinguish fact from fiction – and indeed, for over 200 years scholars in the Western world have been engaged in what has been termed the 'Historical Jesus Quest', but there is not yet any agreed consensus on what it has told us, beyond some broad strokes, which I have outlined above. Nevertheless, almost every scholar, or school of scholarship, has its own favoured theory about what Jesus' main teachings were, what they meant, which stories are probably historical, which less so, and so forth. Indeed, in as far as there is any scholarly consensus, it is the recognition that it is simply impossible to find or identify with 100% accuracy the historical layers of stories from the legendary ones, as the two are entwined and overlapping, while historical narratives are used for particular ideological purposes – they tell a story. Indeed, when people came to write about the lives of figures like Jesus and the Buddha, both they and their audience knew that partly it was a created narrative built up to reflect on those figures (see Box 3.2).

Box 3.2

Making up history?
We need to remember how history was written in ancient times. Even the great Roman historians created speeches that they believed fitted the context or the speaker, and the same was done by the biographers of Jesus – it is no more dishonest or making fairy tales than someone narrating the contemporary lives of Augustus (63 BCE–14 CE) or Claudius (11 BCE–54 CE). All these 'biographies' had elements created by the writer that they thought would be likely or make sense of the narrative.

Divine figures?

What is clear is that all of the world's great religious leaders, as well as philosophers and others, left an impression that made their followers gather stories and narratives that would bring others to their teachings. What is also clear is that each leader was a human being who was eulogized by their followers, and often gained a supernatural aura over time. Certainly, for many religious leaders these are people who, for their followers, mediated absolute reality (the divine, the real, the truth, or however they might conceive it) to them in ways they found to be uniquely compelling. Therefore, it is not surprising that they were often attributed with supernatural powers or even seen as divine in some way. We must not forget that many monarchs were seen as God's regent on earth, and some were seen, and even worshipped, as deities. This is a context where every Roman emperor would be expected to perform miracles, and we see this in their contemporary biographies. Today we often distinguish between attitudes to Jesus and the Buddha by their followers, where they are seen (respectively) as divine and human; however, the distinction is not so clear. We know that many of Jesus' earliest followers saw him as human, and for hundreds of years a branch of Christianity extolling this existed alongside what became orthodox Christianity; just as some of those known generally as the Gnostics denied that Jesus had any human form at all, seeing him instead as a divine manifestation. The former views are recorded in the Bible itself, for the Acts of the Apostles records the saying that Jesus was 'a man attested to you by God' (Acts 2.22). Indeed, amongst the Gospels, only that of John appears to have a divinized Jesus in any form, while contemporary scholarship, which takes attention of the Jewish context, understands Paul's letters as not representing a divine Jesus but rather a human teacher, even if one greatly exalted in the scheme of things. It is noteworthy that from the Reformation onwards, as people started to read the Bible in their own languages as it began to be translated from Latin (the only form that was allowed in medieval Europe), a reading of Jesus as simply human once again became part of the Christian tradition. As such, it is far from a modern liberal attitude.

Comparable in some ways, some of the early records we seem to have of the Buddha portray him as going beyond a normal human state. His first disciples see him and realize he is changed. Also, as the Buddha is on route to see them, he meets another wandering ascetic who seeks to fathom what type of being he might be. Probably somewhat later, stories record him as saying, at the time of his death, that he has transcended his body so need not actually die if he chooses not to die. Later, in parts of the Mahayana tradition, the Buddha is seen as a human manifestation of eternal Buddha Nature. As such, it is wrong to simply contrast a Buddha who taught he was human, and who the tradition sees as human, with a Jesus that Christianity has taught is divine. Today, aspects of both traditions look to the historical records, which show that each figure was seen and understood as human; for example, there is a recorded saying of the Buddha that he was simply human and that anyone could attain what he had attained. That Jesus left nothing comparable is partly due to context: as a devout Jew it would have been blasphemous that anyone could imagine him as divine; but as his early followers developed their traditions in a Greco-Roman world, mainly as non-Jewish converts to whom divine men and demi-gods were a natural part of their world views, it became normal to think of him this way (see Box 3.3).

Box 3.3

Sons and daughters of God

Some claim that the title 'Son of God', which is applied to Jesus in the Gospels shows that the writers thought he was divine. However, this entirely misunderstands the Jewish context. All Jews would see themselves as sons and daughters of God. Sometimes it was used for specifically important people, like prophets, kings or others who were declared specifically a Son of God (so used with capitals as a title). But nowhere in the Jewish tradition did this imply the person so named was divine. A comparable phrase, 'Son of Man', is also used, but it is very likely, as recent research shows, that this was a colloquial phrase meaning something like 'the man in the street' or 'this guy here'. However, in later Christianity, as it became divorced from its Jewish roots, both phrases were understood to mean that Jesus was divine. Likewise, the title Hebrew Messiah, the Greek equivalent of which is the Christ, simply means anointed one (generally, anointing was having oil placed on your forehead, which was a sign of kingship, amongst other things) and does not imply divinity in the Jewish context. Read in a first-century Jewish context, many things in the New Testament, which through Christian culture seem to speak of Jesus' divinity actually do not do so.

One founder who has not been portrayed as divine by his followers, partly explained by the context, is Muhammad. Islam understands itself as following in the tradition of Judaism and Christianity, and so the important figures of those religions are seen as its prophets as well, which includes Abraham, David, Moses and Jesus. Indeed, in setting itself in this lineage, Islam also contested parts of those traditions. In relation to Christianity, this meant arguing that Jesus' followers had misunderstood his message and so had made Jesus into a divine figure by mistake. For Muslims, the idea that God could have a literal son was seen as bizarre, if not abhorrent: it made God simply a creature capable of reproduction and not a being of absolute transcendent reality. Islam's foundational narrative, therefore, sets out that Muhammad is clearly just human and contests the idea that a human being can be divine. (Christians deny that Jesus' sonship implies any physical relation or dividing the distinction between God and humanity.) Generally, this is a pattern found in the monotheisms (i.e. Christianity, Islam and Judaism) of the Middle East where a great gulf is seen between the human and divine realms, whereas in the religious worlds of India and China, although a distinction is often drawn, there are many currents which make the borderline between the human and divine realms less clear-cut.

Contested figures

A lot of contestation surrounds these figures both in the meeting with each other, as well as with atheism. We have discussed some of this, but it would be useful to say a bit more about some specific issues. First, we may note that some have doubted whether Jesus or the Buddha ever existed. Because of historical contexts, more ink has been spilt over the question of Jesus' existence, but there are no credible reasons to believe these figures did not exist, despite that a number of atheist polemicists have made such claims. However, such opinions are not generally accepted by any credible academic authority, historian or scholar (see Box 3.1). With the Buddha we go back around half a millennium and have much later written life stories; however, academic historians find no reason to doubt his existence given the nature of similar historical sources. Turning briefly to the issue of external sources talking about these figures, generally it would take decades or hundreds of years for their traditions to develop to become significant enough that anyone outside the tradition would bother to mention them. In Jesus' case the fact that the Jewish historian Josephus (37–100 CE) gives passing reference to the death of James, mentioned as Jesus' brother, is quite significant in historical terms. While some critics have dismissed this as fabricated because Christian scribes clearly tampered with the texts, this just shows an ignorance of what the evidence is and how to use sources. One reason we know that Christian scribes later tampered with the source is because there is a passage which clearly praises Jesus and on which scholarly opinion is mixed as to whether it is genuine; however, the passage which mentions Jesus and James is just coincidental as background to another story and mentions Jesus as merely 'called the Christ' which is not the way a Christian would have written this, unlike the more dubious passage. In relation to the Buddha, we lack similar testimony, but we have records relating to the Emperor Ashoka (c. 304–232 BCE) about the number and growth of Buddhist schools which takes us back closer, but once again we are dealing with a time when almost all records were oral, not written, and so a lack of sources is not evidence against anyone existing. With Muhammad (c. 570–632), because of the context of the spread of Islam by the united Arab tribes, we get quite a lot of external attestation to his existence from contemporary sources.

Even though we may be clear these figures existed, atheists may still be asking two questions: one is why should it matter to them, and also whether we should revere these figures given that they may be seen in some ways as unsavoury characters. I will address the former point to some extent in the final section of this chapter but address the latter point now. Here we find that many people today, whether religious or not, have respect for Jesus as an ethical teacher and the Buddha likewise for his ethics and meditational teachings. The character of the Prophet Muhammad is, however, much more challenged both by atheists and members of other religions, at least in Europe and America. Indeed, this is not simply a new issue but one which has been there throughout the Western reception of him. It is utterly divergent from how Islamic traditions remember him, where he is described as 'a mercy to the world (universe)', as never losing his temper and being gracious, kind and merciful. We should be aware that in dealing with this I am not attempting to provide a balanced approach to what we may know about the character of Muhammad from the life narratives we have of him; rather, I am responding to what are primarily Christian and atheist representations that have focused on perceived negative aspects. I mention both Christian and atheist because while these are often core arguments of some atheists against Muslims today, they are ones which find their origins in medieval Christian polemic against Islam, often based in the fear and ignorance that existed then. I will address two main questions: Was he a paedophile, and was he a warmonger?

The former criticism is levelled against Muhammad in a number of recent sources; however, little analysis is made of this. The allegation relates to one of his wives, Aisha, who we know was a child when they first became betrothed. But before coming to this, I will briefly address Muhammad's *many* wives. Muhammad's first wife, Khadija, was a successful businesswoman, reportedly around 15 years older than him, and he was one of her employees when they wed. It seems to have been a stable marriage, and while she was alive, he did not take any other wives. Amongst Muhammad's later wives, the majority were widows of Muslims, and following traditional customs, were married to those who would look after them. (In a very different society than we live in today, this was perhaps a practical necessity.) Aisha was the daughter of one of his companions, Abu Bakr, and the marriage was probably more about political union. It is recorded that for the first years they were married, Aisha lived as a child within Muhammad's household and was treated as such; therefore, it was a number of years before the marriage was consummated. We do not actually know at what age the consummation took place; birth certificates did not exist, so people either used community memory or guessed. As such, one traditional recorded age, found in a much later account, that she was nine years old is not reliable; indeed, estimates have put her anywhere from nine to 19 years old. However, in Arab society at that time – indeed, in almost every pre-modern culture – adulthood and the onset of puberty were considered as identical. It is also noteworthy that our contemporary notions of childhood are very modern, and such concepts have been culturally variable. It is quite likely, therefore, that the consummation happened at that time; indeed, in Islamic law it would not be seen as legitimate to be married prior to puberty. This is certainly far younger than we would consider adulthood today, but this was a norm 1000 years ago. In fact, as late as the eighteenth century in England, the age of marriage was officially set at 12 years, while the age of consent to have sexual intercourse with a girl was ten years old. Puberty and sexual maturity, adulthood and marriageable age were basically intertwined. Whether we regard this as desirable or not, we have problems imposing our norms back onto a situation over 1000 years ago, unless we wish to suggest that almost every adult before the past 100 or so years was a paedophile.

My note about eighteenth-century England is not alone, as the government of the French Revolution at the end of that century raised the legal age of marriage from 12 to 13 years for girls. Furthermore, the legal age of marriage for boys was generally higher, reflecting a later reaching of puberty, and had been 14 years in both France and England in that period, raised to 15 years by the revolutionary government. While many Muslims accept the dating that Muhammad first slept with Aisha when she was nine years old (which, as noted, is far from reliable, and in all probability she was older), if so, it indicates that puberty came early, and from a historical point of view, this means Muhammad consummated his marriage to Aisha when she became an adult within her society, that is, it was regarded as a consensual relationship between two legal adults (as far as we can make out). That some Muslims (but by no means all) today understand Muhammad's example as providing a justification for marrying off their nine-year-old daughters is, though, certainly a problem in the contemporary context. (We will discuss this at the end of this chapter and return to gender issues in Chapter 6.)

Our second issue is whether Muhammad was a warmonger. Notably, when Christians responded to Islam from the early centuries, this was a criticism they raised (although nobody in the period raised the previous one we discussed). As noted, in medieval times it would just have been considered normal. Especially when contrasted with figures like Jesus and the Buddha, or even Confucius, the Sikh Guru Nanak or many others, Muhammad is often said to be the only religious founder who fought and advocated violence. (The issue of violence in religions is discussed in Chapter 5.)

In his early life, Muhammad was a merchant, and after the initial set of what he understood as his revelations from God, he started to preach and gather followers, and so he became what we may term a 'religious teacher'. We know that, after a while, as his movement started to spread, the authorities in Mecca started to persecute the nascent Islamic community. At that time, it seems that Muhammad simply advocated a peaceful response. Against this backdrop, Muhammad took his heavily persecuted community to another city, Medina, where his charisma and skills as a negotiator, as well as his religious teachings, saw him becoming a leader within that city. At that point, he was no longer simply a teacher of ethical and spiritual practices but also had duties we may term political, in terms of overseeing the communal life of the city. As such, when war with Mecca ensued, Muhammad led the Medina/Muslim army in the war. Many Muslims assert that it was a defensive war as Mecca first attacked Medina, and so the eventual victory which saw Muhammad take control of both cities was only an outcome of this. However, as part of the historical record, the Meccan offensive seems partly provoked by attacks upon their trading caravans by the Medina community. Such raiding, though, was not especially aggressive; in historical terms, it was not an unusual activity for a particular community. (It was comparable, in some ways, to the licences that England's Queen Elizabeth I gave to privateers to attack Spanish treasure galleons.) Pointing out that Muhammad was a warrior leader in a way that Jesus or the Buddha were not seems a legitimate contrast; however, to suggest that his community was inherently or unusually aggressive is not. At the same time, though, it cannot be claimed that he only ever fought in self-defence. In subsequent centuries Islam would spread rapidly with the expansion of an Arab-Muslim empire, and so the accusation of him being a warmonger probably has more to do with fear amongst his neighbours, primarily Christians in Europe, of a new empire.

THINKING ABOUT RELIGIOUS LEADERS TODAY

With a historical eye, it is quite clear that all the great religious founders were human beings who taught, within the context of their day, a way to what they understood to be absolute reality: for Jesus and Muhammad, a devotional path to God; for the Buddha, the path to awakening. Does this mean that we should simply regard the stories about them as fanciful mythology? Are they little different from fairy tales and just things that may have amused or enticed our forebears but of no meaning to us now? If we took such an attitude, we might miss the fact that the authors of these stories were often creative artists and writers of intricate narratives. As mentioned above, the stories we have today are a complex mix of historical fact, teachings, ideology, historical recreation and mythological elements, but which become part of the whole narrative. As such, to understand these people and their stories may mean to try to read the stories at a more sophisticated level, that is, to try to understand (a) what the writer wants to tell us, (b) why they have included, or excluded, certain elements and (c) what the message being conveyed is. Of course, we could ignore these figures saying we cannot know anything about them, but if we assume that they are figures who have been seen as great spiritual leaders and that these are the narratives that have drawn and still today draw people to them, then perhaps they contain elements we can learn from and appreciate. Religion is not simply a fairy tale, but rather contains philosophy, psychology and even social and political commentary.

There is also another side, and even if we regard many of these figures to have had a significant message or great insights, there are also parts of their message or behaviour which we may not find so conducive to that. While I have mentioned two examples concerning Muhammad, this is not to suggest that he is more problematic than the others; rather, it reflects that these are common issues thrown – even if polemically – into the debate today. But, likewise, many feminists (including Buddhist feminists) are troubled by the fact that the Buddha left his own wife and newly born son, or that Jesus apparently was an eschatological prophet, that is, he believed that God was bringing about the end of the world in his lifetime, which clearly did not happen. All of these figures were human beings who made mistakes. Such a claim is, naturally, antithetical to many of the religious traditions: the figures are either understood as divine, divinely inspired or having transcendental wisdom and therefore beyond error. Progressive religious movements, though, like atheism, have realized that historical facts lead us in another direction. As discussed in Chapter 2, it is known today that what we see as the scriptural books of every religious tradition have a history and are human products, and we need to take a similar attitude to the leaders. Being inspired by them does not mean accepting everything they did. All our heroes have clay feet. Gandhi is one example. While his doctrines of non-violence (*ahimsa*) and pleas to stop oppression against India's underclass of so-called untouchables has inspired many, he also has critics. The untouchables themselves felt patronized by Gandhi's portrayal of them as '*harijans*' (meaning 'children of God') believing his approach simply romanticized them. Furthermore, he was opposed by another leader of Indian independence called Bhimrao Ramji Ambedkar (1891–1956), who demanded more radical political change to alter their status. His plans, though, were thwarted by Gandhi, who undertook a fast to the death if Ambedkar insisted on such reforms. The untouchables today generally take the name Ambedkar gave them (indeed, he was *one* of them): 'Dalit', meaning 'broken' or 'crushed'. This is just one example, but many more could be cited.

When we come to consider what way we think about religious founders today, we can recognize such things as the inspiring example they provided and the ethics they taught, but also recognize that they were human. Nevertheless, it would be hard to relate everything they did, which may have been suited to their time and place, to today's society. In some ways, this provides a greater challenge to those within the religions who have been brought up, or converted, into traditions which often understand these people as irreproachable. We do, of course, see similar worship of figures like this today, whether they be religious leaders, professional athletes or even atheist spokespeople whose words are often imbued with a great sense of authority or factuality. For instance, while Christopher Hitchens no doubt made many good points about the problems with religious traditions, some who admire him even accept his very fallacious arguments that Jesus or the Buddha never existed, which goes against all the available historical evidence and any balanced assessment. For others, their heroes may be professional athletes, media stars or idolized politicians like the USA's John F. Kennedy (1917–1963), Singapore's Lee Kuan Yew (1923–2015) or China's Mao Zedong (1893–1976; also spelt Tsetung; see Box 3.4). We all have a tendency to believe the words of those we admire, but if we also value truth, then we need to be ready to question *any* source, no matter how reliable it seems, when we find better evidence or sources. We should not simply talk about dismissing religion as naive, or about credible people following charismatic leaders; rather, we are looking at the way that we see human activity working, where people and their life stories become embedded in narratives that offer meaning to others. This can be as true of atheists as it can of followers of any religion, and with it there is also a tendency to look to certain figures who are seen to embody or tell those stories.

Box 3.4

Chairman Mao Zedong as God?

In traditional Chinese folk religion, many historical figures have been deified and have joined the pantheon of deities. This process seems to be ongoing, and even the legacy of the atheist leader Chairman Mao Zedong has become part of this. Scholars of Chinese religions have noted the tendency to venerate Mao. Is it likely that the same process will take place with other much-revered contemporary atheist Asia leaders such as Singapore's Lee Kuan Yew?

4

GOD, GODS AND REALITY

THE SCHOLARLY BIT

Many people associate religion with belief in God, an all-powerful creator deity actively involved in the world; however, this is far from typical of every religion. Moreover, even when religions do have some form of absolute deity it is conceived in different ways, sometimes in personal forms as a loving father or mother and other times as an impersonal force or energy, or even as 'Nothing' yet the ultimate source of all things. It may be useful if we outlined a bit of terminology first and where the different religions stand in relation to them. The main terms we will consider are monotheism, polytheism, deism, pantheism, panentheism, henotheism, non-theism and atheism/agnosticism.

Types of 'theism'
Monotheism

Monotheism is the belief that there is a single deity who is the all-powerful (omnipotent), all-knowing (omniscient) and all-loving (omnibenevolent) creator. It is found in the three so-called Abrahamic religions (Christianity, Islam and Judaism), but also in Hinduism. Most Hindus belong to one of three main traditions: Shaivism, followers of the god Shiva; Vaishnavism, followers of the god Vishnu (often in the form of Krishna or Rama); and Shaktism, followers of the goddess often known as Devi (or Mahadevi, literally 'Great Goddess'), Durga, Kali or other names. The other gods and goddesses are simply manifestations of this one deity in different forms. In Hindu thought this supreme deity is generally seen as personal (associated with *dvaita*/dualist philosophy: the deity and humanity are distinct), but there is also a school of thought which says the supreme is ultimately impersonal (*advaita*/non-dualist: deity and the human are one).

Polytheism

Polytheism is belief in many deities and was found amongst the ancient Greeks, Romans, Egyptians, Celts and many others. It is also the belief of many Hindus in rural areas and amongst the tribal groups in India who see their deities as distinct. It is probably what is found in the most ancient Vedic texts, Hinduism's oldest scriptures.

Deism

Deism is the belief that there is a creator deity, but that either this deity is impersonal or simply uninterested in the creation. As such the deist believes that deity sets things in motion but leaves us alone to live as we see fit. It became popular amongst a number of philosophical thinkers in Europe and North America associated with what may be termed 'rational religion' during the Enlightenment period. It explained the problem of evil (discussed further below) when many could not imagine how the world existed without a creator (see Chapter 7).

Pantheism

Pantheism is the belief that the world, or universe, is infused with some spiritual essence such that God is essentially the world or cosmos and not distinct from it. The divine is not conceived as something outside the world but simply as part of the natural process. It was popularized as a philosophical concept by the philosopher Baruch Spinoza (1632–1677) and is found today amongst a number of contemporary Pagan groups in the West.

Panentheism

Panentheism (note the extra 'en' in relation to Pantheism) is a belief that God cannot be spoken of as separate and distinct from the world but also transcends it. As such, God is not simply the world or universe but more than that. In this sense, it is akin to a form of monotheism where there is a supreme reality, but rather than stressing the distinction of this supreme reality from all creation, it is emphasized that deity is totally bound up in, and dwells within, everything which emanates from the divine; hence, deity is emphasized as being imminent (within and inside the self and creation), rather than transcendent (beyond and outside the self and creation). While the term has only recently been coined, many forms of monotheism, at least as expounded by some theological or philosophical teachers, are akin to it. It is often associated with what are termed 'mystical expressions' of many religions; examples include spiritual writer Meister Eckhart (c. 1260–1328), various Islamic Sufi thinkers and some Kabbalistic Jews. Likewise, many Hindu theologians seem inclined to this standpoint which can be justified in many of the Upanishads, important philosophical texts included in the Vedas.

Henotheism

Henotheism is the belief that while there are many gods, one of them is the supreme deity who exceeds all others. It is distinct from polytheism where there may be a king or chief god by emphasizing that only this one should be worshipped. In this form it seems to typify much ancient Israelite religion where the Hebrew Bible speaks about Yahweh as the supreme deity but does not discount others. It may also typify some early Hindu thought.

Non-theism

Non-theism is a term that can be used for traditions like Buddhism. While I have mentioned above that many Western Buddhists understand Buddhism to be atheist, it clearly has not been so in most forms throughout history (unless we define atheism narrowly as simply disbelief in the monotheists' deity). The early Buddhist scriptures do not deny that the Hindu deities exist; it merely topples them from the supreme position. In traditional Buddhist thought, the gods are simply like all other sentient beings (i.e. all creatures: humans, animals, ghosts, demons, angels and deities), which will die and be reborn as part of the realm of impermanence. As such, for monastics the gods were effectively of no importance. Unlike Christianity, where the deity was the source of salvation, for monastics the gods were simply a distraction – themselves caught in the realm of *samsara* (the cycle of rebirth characterized by ignorance, greed and anger). Lay Buddhists, however, would frequently pray to the gods for good harvests, luck in marriage or business, and so forth. Some forms of Buddhism (especially the Mahayana tradition) came to speak of celestial Buddhas who lived in heavenly realms, and also Bodhisattvas (beings who could assist on the path to awakening), in god-like ways. These beings were understood as either a type of ideal archetype or effectively divine. Some modern Western Pagan traditions, including some goddess traditions, see the deities about which they speak as being just useful ideas or inspirational archetypes, not necessarily emphasizing whether they are real or not. These people may identify explicitly as atheist Pagans.

Atheism

Atheism is the belief that there is no deity nor any kind of transcendent reality. In this it contrasts with the agnostic who says there is not enough evidence either way or is not certain. Many atheists will assert that atheism is actually not a 'belief' – even that it is the opposite of 'belief'. However, as discussed in Chapter 1, this is really about semantics (i.e. what we consider words to mean or imply), and I use it here to talk about world views just as we talk about political, philosophical or ethical beliefs. Of course, some may give no thought to whether God exists, and so it doesn't seem a position *per se*, yet in as far as it is discussed, it holds the status of a 'belief' about the world in a general sense. Lawrence Krauss, for instance, has said that God's existence is a notion to which he and other scientists simply give no thought (however, he seems to spend a lot of time debating and arguing about it for someone who gives it no thought!). Also, as noted in Chapter 1, the idea that scientists aren't religious is not a global norm.

Three issues for further discussion

These convenient 'theism' categories do not necessarily exhaust all the options. Dutch scholars have recently coined a new term, 'Ietism', which refers to those people who believe there is something but do not know, or care enough, to enquire what it is. Perhaps we could think of it in Hamlet's words: 'There are more things in heaven and on earth, Horatio, Than are dreamt of in your philosophy'.

There are several issues to discuss: first, whether it is possible to prove or disprove the existence of a deity over which many words have been spilt in human history; second, the problem of evil, that is, whether the typical god of monotheism (i.e. the one who is omnibenevolent, omniscient and omnipotent) is compatible with the evil which exists; and third, the relationship between the different 'theisms' (including atheism).

Arguments for God

For anyone interested in the classical arguments for and against the existence of God, there are many excellent texts and overviews, especially in the discipline known as the philosophy of religion where they tend to be located within the contemporary intellectual debate. As such, I will not rehearse them in any detail here; however, I will briefly touch on them as they are relevant to the development of our discussion.

We start in the eighteenth century with the man generally credited with having shown that arguments for the existence of God were setting out on an impossible journey: Immanuel Kant (1724–1804). Kant stands as one of the most important figures not simply in the history of philosophy, but also in the whole story of modernity and the Enlightenment. In 1784 he wrote a very famous article entitled 'What is Enlightenment?'. In it he spelt out many important principles which are worth quoting (in a very colloquial translation):

> Enlightenment is getting out of the childhood that you've kept yourself in. Mentally, you're still a minor if you can't use your mind without having someone else tell you what and how to think. This is your own fault if the problem is not that you have the bad luck to be retarded or brain-damaged, but that you just can't make up your own mind and are afraid to use your brains without someone else

dictating what you think. *Sapere aude! Dare to know!* 'Have the guts to use your own wits,' is thus the slogan of the Enlightenment.

'Dare to know' is a motto of the whole Enlightenment, a movement which challenged traditional authorities, whether this was the churches, monarchies or the aristocracy. Part of the established views that Kant attacked was the idea that we could know that God existed. He made a distinction between the phenomenal, which is the physical world with which we interact, and the noumenal, which is the realm of the transcendent. The former, he said, we could know, whereas the latter we could not interact with using our senses, and so any claims to know it must be open to dispute and challenge. Kant therefore dismissed all the traditional arguments for the existence of God. (Note, however, that Kant did not think we were limited to only our sense knowledge and endeavoured to develop a moral argument for God's existence; for his refutation of the Ontological Argument, see Box 4.1.)

Box 4.1

The Ontological Argument

The so-called Ontological Argument goes back at least to Anselm of Canterbury (c. 1033–1109) and is often simplified as follows: deity is the greatest conceivable idea; something that exists is greater than something that doesn't; the greatest deity would exist; therefore that deity exists. This does not do justice to Anselm's thought, which is actually very philosophically interesting and raises questions about the nature of logic, argumentation and existence. Note that it was also not advanced to prove God existed to sceptics, but was part of a meditation on the nature of the deity. Despite this, it has been 'disproven' several times, often by Christian philosophers like Aquinas and Kant. Kant's refutation of the Ontological Argument was quite subtle, but in part he used a simple analogy: take a pile of 100 coins; whether they are real or imaginary, they have the same value; therefore, adding existence does not make one pile of coins 'greater'. Despite such refutations, it has fascinated thinkers, including the atheist philosopher Bertrand Russell (1872–1970) who is said to have cried out one day 'Great God in boots, the Ontological Argument works!' while on his way to buy tobacco. Accepting it as a logical argument did not, of course, make Russell a theist, any more than the theist Kant saw his refutation as a disproof of God.

Since Kant's time, theologians and philosophers have disputed the sharp distinction he made, but there has often been a general consensus that any argument for God's existence is impossible, although throughout the twentieth century and into the twenty-first many arguments for God's existence have once again become serious and live areas of debate. Part of this has come from looking at cosmology, and theoretical physicists have claimed there may be some form of 'design' built into the universe. Having said this, many contemporary disputations for God's existence tend to lack much intellectual credibility, especially in terms of the design argument. Readers may be aware of a Christian apologist named Roy Comfort who has attempted to revive the design argument by suggesting that various aspects of the world suggest God's existence, and he is perhaps most famous for the one which has seen him dubbed 'banana man' by Richard Dawkins. He argued that because it was convenient to peel and changed colour when ripe, the banana proved a 'designer', although he didn't seem to consider coconuts or the durian fruit as possible disproofs! (We discuss design further in relation to the relationship of religion and science in Chapter 7.)

The flip side of the argument that any deity belongs in a noumenal realm, to use Kant's language, is also that a disproof is not possible. As such, Kant's position could be seen as having advantages and disadvantages to both sides of the argument. Nevertheless, this is not to say that we may not have good reasons to suppose that any deity is either more or less likely to exist, or even that some conceptions of such a deity (or reasons for the non-existence of any deity) are more reasonable than others. We will discuss one significant aspect of this shortly, the problem of evil, but first we need to discuss religious experiences.

Religious experiences

For many religious people, one often cited 'sure proof' that a deity exists is that they have had some direct and personal experience: for evangelical Protestants, this is often the Risen Jesus appearing in their life; for Pentecostals, it is more likely the Holy Spirit; for Catholics, appearances are often of the Virgin Mary. Likewise, members of other religious traditions may experience in some way a host of other figures or have some form of 'mystical experience' of the ineffable, as do many of what are termed Christian mystics. Of course, the immediate rebuttal from atheists is twofold: first, such experiences are capable of being explained in terms of hallucinations, or even some form of brain activity; and second, a critique that goes back to at least the Scottish philosopher David Hume (1711–1776), although he used miracles as his example of competing claims, is the fact that because every religion makes its own, seemingly incompatible, claims counts against the likelihood of any one being true.

I would like to make a few points before discussing this further: First, these experiences are often of a type that may be described as 'overpowering', being of a nature unlike anything previously experienced. Therefore, for those who experience them, they seem uniquely real and self-authenticating. Second, this 'overpoweringness' is, of course, no guarantee of their veracity; however, it does mean that trying to tell people that they are not 'real' is very difficult. Third, within religious narratives there are ways to make sense of the religious experiences of other religions, either 'negatively' as demonic temptations or falsehood, or 'positively' as the deity is seen to be accessible to all people at all times. (This latter point is not simply a modern liberal interpretation as many suppose, but has been held within pretty much all religions; we discuss this further in Chapter 8.) Finally, even if such experiences relate to a brain-state or can be explained in naturalistic ways, it is, of course, not proof that this is all that they are. This doesn't mean that it becomes feasible to explain them in theistic terms, but various interpretations *are* possible. One of the most important interpretations of religious experiences was that of the sociologist and anthropologist Émile Durkheim (1858–1917). He argued that the experiences of some 'spiritual' power that he studied in indigenous tribes were not simply fantasy; rather, he surmised, they were a result of a communal ecstasy (a word which literally means going outside of yourself), where the rituals and beliefs of the group led to a heightened state that transcended any individual. Meanwhile, recent studies in neurology have shown that certain parts of the brain tend to be activated by different forms of prayer or meditation; however, here, our interest is not in the experiences themselves (which are fascinating but would require a major study to do them justice, but we discuss this further in Chapter 8), but rather how they relate to any belief in a deity. What we need to take away is that despite many agreeing with Kant that knowledge or understanding of the noumenal is inaccessible to human enquiry does not mean that everyone agrees that the deity remains unknown, because it is argued that the experience is possible (a stance held in most religious traditions).

We should note, in terms of theological speculation, many religions have argued that the deity or transcendent reality is ultimately unknown and cannot be expressed by human language (see Box 4.2). That, for most religions, the deity or the ultimate is capable of experience but unknowable is taken by some atheists as a sign that discourse about the deity may be meaningless. So, this is a good time to discuss the thing that for many most clearly makes discussions of God meaningless: suffering.

Box 4.2

The via negativa and analogy

The idea that whatever God, the absolute, divine or transcendent reality may be, cannot be encapsulated within the limits of human language has been common in many religions. In the Christian West this has been known by the Latin term *via negativa* (literally 'the way of negation'). It suggests that even positive human terms like 'love' or 'goodness' do not apply, because the words refer only to what humans can imagine, which cannot encapsulate the sheer magnitude of whatever ultimate reality may be. Another trend, championed by Aquinas in the Christian West, who thought the *via negativa* went too far, is analogy, such that words like 'love', while inadequate, at least point us in the right direction. However, some theologians have claimed even 'positive' phrases, such as 'God exists', are misleading. To say God exists, it is argued, is to say that God is a *thing* like many others in the universe, but if deity is above and beyond all other things, it may be better to say God doesn't exist, not as an atheist statement but to help break down our ways of conventional thinking. In Indian philosophy such negation has a long tradition in what is often seen as a pattern of multiple negations and affirmations, so we could say: it is true; it is not true;

it is both true and not true; it is neither true nor not true. This seems odd to Western philosophers who stress the law of non-contradiction: every statement must be either true or false – it cannot be both. But consider the statement: this statement is false. If it is true, then it contradicts itself; if false, then it makes itself true. As such, Indian philosophy and its inheritors have suggested that we should not be afraid of seeming paradoxes or contradictions. The Buddhist philosopher Nagarjuna (c. first to second century CE) employed a variant in what is often called the eightfold negation of being that things have: no arising; no ending; no permanence; no extinction; no self-identity; no difference; no coming; no going. Such language offers very traditional and sophisticated ways within religious traditions to speak about (or not speak about) what is seen as transcendent or unknown, and far from being simply obscurantist is actually part of a very sophisticated philosophical tradition of argumentation and linguistic analysis. It is found across religions: Gregory of Nazianzus (329–390) and Meister Eckhart (1260–1328) in Christianity; Al-Ghazali (1058–1111) and Rumi (1207–1273) in Islam; and is expressed poetically in the Daoist Daodejing: 'The Dao that can be expressed is not the eternal Dao, the Name that can be named is not the eternal name'.

The problem of evil

The problem of evil is not a new concern. We know that within the Israelite tradition it is quite ancient, going back to the discussion in the Book of Job in the Bible (c. 2000–1000 BCE). Here a man named Job who is seen as righteous is allowed to be attacked by the devil. (Notably, in this ancient story, the devil does not appear as a figure in hell, or God's adversary, but someone in the court of heaven, as the tempter sent by God; the history of this figure has been written elsewhere.) The story raises questions about why innocent people suffer and what their response should be, although the answer in the story is basically that the deity created all things and is supremely powerful, so what right has a meagre human to question the almighty! Not everyone has been satisfied with this answer, and it has given rise to the theological field of theodicy – attempts to explain suffering.

Classically stated, the problem of evil goes like this: if God is all-loving but unable to end suffering, then he is not all-powerful, and if God is able to end suffering but unwilling to do so, then he is not all-loving. Christian theodicies make various answers to this. One of the most famous is known as the Irenaen Theodicy, after an early Christian writer called Irenaeus (c. 120/140 to 200–203 CE), was given a strong defence by the philosopher of religion, John Hick (1922–2012). The argument suggests that if we lived in a world where there was no suffering we would neither learn nor have morality; if hitting people with swords didn't kill them, there would be no injunction *not* to kill, and neither could we learn love and compassion in response to the suffering of others. Therefore, there *must* be evil in the world, because it is only in relation to evil that we can know good. Just as we can have no sense of light without dark, or heat without cold. We therefore live in a world of 'soul making', where we can and do make moral choices and can become good people by making the right kinds of choices; hence, this is often called the Soul Making Theodicy.

Critics counter, however, that the level of suffering in this world exceeds what we would need to make moral choices, and sometimes seems quite unjust and gratuitous. Several responses have been made to this:

- Our idea that there is too much suffering is relative; for instance, if you had only ever experienced a mildly sore throat as the worst pain, then suddenly cutting your thumb might seem unbearably excruciating, while if there was not suffering that seems unbearable to us (with our relative sense of what pain is), then moral choices would be weakened. If the worst pain was only moderate, or people bounced back after dying, we would never face hard moral choices (i.e. a cartoon world cannot be a moral world).

- Whatever suffering is experienced here will seem as nothing compared with the infinite pleasure and joys of heaven. As such, all human suffering is merely finite and temporary, and would seem as nothing compared with what is gained in the hereafter.

- If there were not seemingly unjust suffering, then we would also lose moral choice, that is, if good people had only good things happen to them, being 'good' would not be a moral choice but one of self-interest, while if only the wicked suffered, then everyone would stop being bad out of self-interest. As such, seemingly unjust suffering and terrible things must happen, in ways that make no sense to us, for us to be able to make moral choices without coercion.

- The pain itself can be good for us. That is, that we build character and fortitude through what we suffer through life, and that if we all lived in an easy world, we would never develop will power, because even if we never tried, no harm would come from it. As such, suffering is its own good. Related to this, some suggest that suffering can help draw people to God, or that if your faith is enough, then you can put up with it, or that God will never give people more than they can bear. (Of course, there are also counterarguments to these viewpoints.)

It is sometimes pointed out that some of the suffering is just so gratuitous and awful that it seems to negate any sense of a higher good or moral agent being the cause (the diseases inflicted on very young infants, for instance). What lessons can be learnt by being born with your internal organs outside your body so that you will die in agony with only limited consciousness? Again, for Voltaire (1694–1778), a philosopher who had been religious but lost his faith, a key incident was the Lisbon earthquake of 1755. In this event an earthquake shook the city and, in the aftermath, many people went to help those caught by the earthquake and the fires it caused. However, a side effect of the earthquake was a tsunami which, several days afterwards, swept over the city and killed not just survivors of the earthquake but also many of those who had gone to help. We mentioned above a system which rewards the good and punishes the bad is argued as not enhancing morality, but Voltaire thought that if this was ordained by some entity, then it must be a monster. In other words, maybe we could see how the earthquake could cause sympathy in people and so have a moral result – despite the suffering – but the subsequent tsunami was simply gratuitous. What good was caused by that event? Indeed, the problem of evil in various forms seems to be one of the main reasons why people lose their faith and become atheists or agnostics.

In the twentieth century, one of the most traumatic events in Europe was the Holocaust. The attempted destruction of Europe's Jewish population, which wiped out many millions of Jews (although we must not forget that the Romany people and other groups were also targeted by the Nazis, and it was far from being the only instance of attempted genocide the world has seen). In the Nazi concentration camps many Jews lost their faith. Elie Wiesel's personal testimony is a compelling account of how he lost his faith witnessing the deaths of women and children. Where was God when such slaughter was occurring? How could it happen if there is a God who answers prayers, cares for his children and is all-loving? It created much soul-searching, not just in Judaism but also in Christianity because the mainstream churches came to realize that they were implicated in the history of anti-Semitism which had led to this event: theological anti-Judaism, charges of deicide (killing God), institutional and societal exclusion and persecution of Jews, and full-blown violent anti-Semitism are all found in 2000 years of Christian history.

In what has been termed post-Holocaust theology, various answers have been given by both Jews and Christians. One response is that it is impossible to believe in a deity after this event, so it leads to atheism. For some, it does not necessarily lead to proclaimed atheism because there may still be a need for some form of spirituality or talk of God, even if not in realist ways. Another response is that belief in a personal God as some kind of heavenly father is impossible, and so a belief in some form of distant deity (deism) was endorsed. For others, God was reinterpreted as some force or energy within the universe, certainly not as all-powerful, or else part of the universal forces in some way – even if a benevolent force (pantheism or panentheism). Another response, certainly amongst Jews, is that to stop believing would be to give Hitler the victory. A final response is to go back to traditions like Job, which is to say that God, while he could intervene often, does not because that would limit human freedom; if the Jews had been miraculously rescued, it would have been clear divine intervention, which would limit free will.

For many people there seems to be a need to believe that if there is evil, then a deity is needed: What kind of universe must it be if only terrible evil exists but no good? How do we live in the world without believing that goodness must eventually win? Despite evil, therefore, belief is sometimes motivated, or has roots, in a desire or need to believe that things can be better. Of course, the atheist may insist that humans can learn to do good and make the world better by their own actions, something with which religious people would often agree.

Certainly, despite the presence of evil and suffering, and even after the Holocaust and other terrible events, the majority of the world's population still has religious faith. Of course, much of it is not in the personal omnibenevolent, omniscient and omnipotent monotheist deity of the Abrahamic traditions that is most at risk from the problem of evil. Buddhism, for instance, generally invokes no creator, and famously, the Buddha refused to enter into discussions of where the world had come from simply by insisting that we are in a world dominated by suffering. (To be more precise, a world of impermanence and our desires for permanence and possession lead us to suffering when we ultimately cannot hold on to what we crave. Note that contrary to many misinterpretations, Buddhism is not a pessimistic way of life, but rather sees itself as being realistic and holding an answer to the problem of impermanence and suffering, i.e. it sees itself as an optimistic world view.) Rather, the Buddha taught that we must find a way out of suffering, a way which involves cultivating compassion towards others as well as purifying one's own mind through meditation.

Many forms of Hinduism present *karma* as an ever-present cosmic law which means that actions and consequences follow from each other. This is not to say that these religions are not without their own issues concerning the problem of evil or solve all the questions that may arise, but certainly they are less threatened in this respect than Christianity, Islam and Judaism. It is not that religious people are unaware of the problem of evil or ignore it; instead, they find ways to reconcile it with their faith. The question remains, though, as to whether this is hiding from the problem or wishful thinking of some kind.

At the very least, any image of God as some kindly father figure in the sky who actively intervenes in the world is deeply destabilized. As an analogy, to speak of God as 'father' we wonder what kind of parent would allow the suffering we see if it could be prevented? For many people who nevertheless have some need, desire or experience of the divine, other choices certainly seem to be more compelling.

This is not the place to discuss in detail such theologies, but for many former traditional monotheists the problem of evil, amongst other issues, may lead them to agnosticism, atheism, Buddhism, a modified belief like panentheism or pantheism found in schools of thought like Process Theology (which sees God not as a creator but a transcendent force within or alongside the universe), or some forms of feminist theology where the deity is spoken of in other ways. For instance, the American theologian Carter Heyward speaks of 'Godding', where instead of being a noun (a 'being' out there), we use the divine as a verb to talk about what happens in the relationship between people: God is therefore found in positive human interrelationships where we can make the world more meaningful. Whatever the case, evil and suffering are one of the greatest challenges faced by religion in its many forms.

Religion and atheism

Having discussed the problem of evil and various religious responses to it, a further issue that arises is what the difference is between various forms of religion and agnosticism, and indeed, also, atheism. As we have seen, religious people have responded to the problem of evil in many ways; indeed, this is not simply since the Holocaust but throughout history. Also, what we call 'religions' have responded to, or reacted to what is called 'the divine', in many different ways. We are not talking about new or modern answers that have been dreamt up to respond to contemporary questions like evil, atheism or science – these have been issues for hundreds or thousands of years in different ways, and religions are very diverse. Some of these ideas may be useful today.

Religions come in different versions: from big-God monotheism to accepting some spiritual reality; from seeing the divine as what happens when we meet to being actually atheist and saying that God talk is metaphorical or perhaps part of an archaic past. In relation to the latter viewpoint, there are secular Jews who (if we think of Judaism religiously rather than ethnically) have a form of atheist Judaism, while there are atheist Christian movements like the Sea of Faith movement in the UK and the USA's 'Death of God' theologians. We may ask, then, what is it that radically distinguishes this from atheism? We may say that it is still wanting to use God language, but this does not seem to be the case. For instance, Auguste Comte (1798–1857) desired to set up a Church of Atheism which would use a religious model. While it didn't take off, there is today a growing interest and participation in the Sunday worship forms of atheism, or atheist churches, a movement which began in the UK but is now found in the USA and other places. Meanwhile, exemplified by books like Alain de Botton's *Religion for Atheists*, we can see many who call themselves atheists but are nevertheless interested in some form of 'spirituality' or, at least, the traditions and language of religion. Botton argues that it has resources to help inform our ideas. We do not, therefore, simply see a sharp contrast between, on the one hand, atheists, and on the other, religious people – it is more of a continuum. When we consider agnostics who may be more or less convinced that there is or is not a deity, then we also see a middle ground. Many Buddhists meanwhile, at least in the West, see their tradition as atheist and will call it an atheist religion, or eschew that term and call it a philosophy or way of life. Indeed, even one of the most prominent of the so-called New Atheists, Sam Harris, has said that he finds a lot of Buddhist ideas very congenial. At a recent gathering of the British Humanist Association, the atheist scholar Tim Whitmarsh quoted approvingly from Pliny the Elder (23–79 CE): 'God is one mortal helping another', which we must admit is very similar to Carter Heyward's concept of Godding mentioned above. One of these figures endorses finding 'the divine' between the meetings of humans, and calls themself an atheist, the other suggests the same and calls themself a theologian and a Christian. Certainly, some may suggest that Whitmarsh has muddied the waters and was unhelpful in his language, and others may say that if this is all Carter thinks is the divine, then she is no longer really Christian nor a theist. Nevertheless, it shows that people identifying with the supposedly different camps may find the language of religion, even the language of God, useful.

Certainly, many religious people, of whom the former Archbishop of Canterbury Rowan Williams is one, have said that part of faith is actually doubt. Things like the problem of evil mean that faith/belief is not a certainty but rather something deeply held that is also something about which doubt exists, or from which you can certainly feel at times you could fall away. Indeed, Williams' successor,

Archbishop Justin Welby, has also spoken of the way suffering has led him to doubts. It also, as we have mentioned, may mean that many religious people find it easier to think of God in terms which do not match the traditional 'omni-deity' (i.e. the all-loving, all-powerful, all-knowing). In such areas there may be closer links between atheists and the religious than is often conceived.

THINKING ABOUT A-/NON-/THEISM TODAY

We have already started to think about ways that these issues can be considered today. The common rhetoric from staunch atheists and avid believers pits the two sides as antithetical camps where the answer is either for or against God, with no middle ground. However, the contemporary context of faith and contemporary atheism are far more complex. Personally, I find anyone who crudely accepts the big and prayer-answering father-in-the-sky model of God to either be hiding from the problem of evil or not to have considered it seriously. I grant, though, that for reasons of finding a personal answer to some pain or suffering, that we should not condemn such belief outright without considering the reasons people hold it. Indeed, I, and I suspect many of my readers, come to this from positions of relative global privilege. But there are countries where medicine or healthcare, and even education, are limited and where such a faith may be an important aspect of people's identity. Even, I think, the staunchest atheist should consider how to approach such people from a world that is very different. Nevertheless, I would suggest that religious people have a duty to share problems they have with such images of deity with others. Envisaging God not as some father in the sky who can grant favours, may help people be more active in helping others – notwithstanding that the belief in such a God has inspired many to acts of service. Indeed, equally I believe that there is no religious case for condemning an atheist who finds evil too great a reason not to believe in God and even to leave behind religion altogether. It may seem that I wish to give support to every position here, which is not necessarily the case. However, I believe that until we know the causes and reasons for any individual's position, we should not judge that person. Religious belief today needs to take the problem of evil very seriously and realize that many of the traditional answers simply come up short. It also shows, against the unfair stereotype of atheism as immoral, that people can adopt this position from a strong personal sense of inner morality that makes them separate themselves from talk of God or religion. Is an atheist who reflects on evil and rejects God because of moral outrage more ethical in outlook than a Christian who simply finds their faith a useful social identity? Which should we see as the moral choice? To be religious today, certainly in the Western world and in other developed countries where people have the time and leisure to be able to consider these issues, means that we should rethink the God question. If God would not spare babies from torture, infants from debilitating diseases and adults from pain and suffering that is often far beyond what they can bear, then there is a problem. Indeed, I think this is why good theological reasons may lead people to alternative positions than belief in a personal deity.

There are reasons linked to what is known as pastoral theology, the care of people. I would like to use as an example from a well-known Christian book called *The Shack* (2007) by William P. Young. In that book the young daughter of a family on holiday is kidnapped by a psychopathic paedophile and is brutally raped and murdered. Going to the place where it occurred, the father meets God and also is allowed to talk to his daughter, which assuages his own guilt in not protecting her, because she tells him that because she loved Jesus so much, the events did not harm or traumatize her, as her faith was so strong. Personally, while there may be some interesting ideas in the book, I find this part of the story quite repellent. The narrative that comes out of this is as follows: if you suffer some harm or abuse and this hurts, affects or traumatizes you in any way, the fault is yours – if your faith was strong enough, then Jesus/God would help you bear it, and you wouldn't be affected. It is hard to imagine what kind of guilt this sort of message – which is not only found in this book but also advocated by certain forms of what is termed 'Christian counselling' propagated by mainly evangelical groups (not to be confused with the kind of trained pastoral care found in other churches, including many evangelical ones who reject such an abusive message) – would give not just to children but many adults who have been through traumatic events. They would have to cope not just with whatever shame or pain they feel from the event, but also the story that their religion or faith does not support them but instead condemns them for even having any problems. Clearly, this form of abusive psychology is not inherently linked to a particular belief in God (and non-religious groups also use similar psychological ploys to gain control over their members), but the notion of a personal intervening God is linked to a storyline in which a failure to secure an intervention from the deity can readily be linked to a personal lack of faith. Different religious or spiritual conceptions, while not free from abuse – as indeed is true of all world views – may nevertheless be beneficial. It is also very understandable why such approaches and attitudes repel people from religion.

There are philosophically theological reasons to reject such a position. First, a particular belief in Christianity, Islam or Judaism today is that God created the universe out of nothing, what is classically termed creation *ex nihilo*. However, it is certainly debatable if such a position is biblical. The concept appears to have arisen in the centuries around the birth of Christianity, beginning a few centuries earlier and developing strongly around its origins. The Book of Genesis, however, tells us that God moved over the face of the deep, or waters (Genesis 1.1), at the beginning of creation. This suggests that the deep (primordial waters – I will explain this in a moment) already existed and that God was simply acting upon what already existed. As is clear historically, much of the early Hebrew Bible owes its origins to existing texts and stories in the Middle East, and in many of them the creator deity does not create *ex nihilo*, but rather acts upon the existing primordial chaos bringing shape to what already exists. Creation is therefore about bringing order to disorder and shaping what is there. This primordial chaos, in the Hebrew Bible and in much ancient Middle Eastern mythology, is associated with water (the oceans, or depths), which is seen to be unknown, unpredictable and dangerous. Hence, the Book of Genesis, rather than containing a story of creation *ex nihilo*, is actually repeating the age-old mythos of ordering the primal chaos.

Attention to the biblical text would therefore lead Christians and Jews at least to a different understanding of their deity – not as the all-powerful creator out of nothing, but simply the force which has ordered chaos to some degree at least. This also provides its own theodicy, because evil in the world can be partly explained as coming from the inherent chaos of the material universe rather than being God's creation; God does not have complete control but acts only upon what is there. For a less theistic spirituality, a force of ordering or benevolence could be seen as something within the universe acting on and through it, rather than as an outside force that creates all things. Of course, from an atheist position it may be said that there is no need for such a hypothesis. (We discuss this further in Chapter 7.)

Second, religions say their deity or transcendent reality is ultimately beyond human understanding (see Box 4.2). While pretty much all institutionalized forms of religion say their language captures God or the divine such that it is best expressed their way, this is always theologically open to question; it is possible to quote authorities in both camps. Therefore, resources exist within Christianity and every major religious tradition for arguing that any anthropomorphic (human-like) image of God is simply a projection of the human mind, which is easy for people to cope with but does not represent the transcendent reality itself. This line is much taken up by the Sufi tradition in Islam, a tradition which has been very influential, although often criticized by mainline institutions, with some Sufis being accused of heresy and even killed. Nevertheless, such narratives provide a strong tradition for arguing that God should not be perceived as some big anthropocentric figure.

Box 4.3

Spirituality

'Spirituality' is a very vague term and sometimes used to mean almost anything, although some Christian writers have noted that it has a particular heritage within their tradition and so should only properly be used to talk about specific Christian activities of prayer and the interior life. I think there are good reasons for seeing it as much broader, and certainly that is how it is often understood today in general usage. This is how I employ it here: without a precise definition but referring to a sense of 'religiosity', or 'connectedness', or 'serenity' generated by particular practices which may be followed without adherence to a particular religious tradition.

Spirituality and inter-being

I say something now about spirituality (see Box 4.3) and inter-being. Many people today identify as spiritual but not religious, often meaning that they have trouble with particular organized forms of religious traditions and the kinds of doctrines they preach. Nevertheless, such people feel they want to connect with some form of what we can generally call religious practice. In some ways this often feeds off what we tend to term the 'spiritual' or 'mystical' trends within religion: such as Sufism in Islam; mystics like Meister, Eckhart (1260–1368), Johannes Tauler (1300–1361), John of the Cross (1542–1591) or contemporary Christian meditation movements within Christianity; streams in Advaita Vedanta, yoga or *bhakti* (devotion) within Hinduism; meditation and mindfulness, especially from Zen traditions, in Buddhism; Daoist teachings and practices; or a network of what are seen as Pagan practices. For some, such practices may be seen as detachable from the religious tradition from which they came and can be used for personal spiritual benefits. However, spirituality is not simply about religious practices, and some scientists have spoken of a sense of wonder or awe, even spirituality, that comes from contemplating the cosmos or the wonders of nature. (Of course, not only scientists have this wonder, as we also see it in poets, philosophers, artists and theologians.) Atheists will also employ meditation or yoga traditions as part of their own practices – whether they see them as religious in any way or not. It is certainly the case, though, that many people who feel they cannot commit to any organized religion still desire a sense of something that is perhaps best summed up by the term 'spirituality'. Whether this is conceived theistically, pan(en)theistically or atheistically, the same sources may be drawn upon.

The term 'inter-being' was coined by Thich Nhat Hanh, a Vietnamese Zen monk who now lives in France at a centre called Plum Village. (He came to prominence during the Vietnam War for his anti-war activism and has subsequently lived mainly in exile encouraging people to spirituality and social activism.) He uses it to talk about traditional religious teachings in a way he sees as relevant to spiritual seekers today, and I provide a rough summary of his extensive ideas here.

Inter-being is about being mindful, which is to be consciously aware of the way our mind works and the often negative thoughts we have even when we think we are acting with good intentions. It is also concerned with the way that we are always connected to other people, such that our thoughts and actions affect others. Some people see spirituality and mysticism as indulging in individualistic personal quests, but as Thich Nhat Hanh emphasizes, this is very different from what religions actually teach: understanding must go hand in hand with compassion. In traditional Buddhist thought, wisdom and compassion are spoken of as two hands that wash each other. Likewise, for Christianity, scholar Grace Jantzen has shown that medieval mystics, like Meister Eckhart, were not simply obsessed with personal mystical ecstasies but actually taught an engaged compassion. Eckhart is quoted as saying that it is better to feed soup to a starving man than to experience some personal revelation of God within yourself. These spiritual traditions have focused not simply on some transcendent experience but on active service and encounter with others. Is this, perhaps, an area where atheists and the religious meet? As someone using theistic language might put it: God is in the meeting place between people. Atheists (and Buddhists) may naturally disavow such theistic language, so we can also say that meaning in the world is the meeting place between people. This rejection of religious language is understandable, and religious people need to realize that there are good reasons for this; one is that it can often be used in abusive ways, as discussed. I have suggested here, though, that we should not see two radically opposed camps, and that while some stand at different poles, there are places where many religious people and atheists may meet in the middle ground, even if some will remain fighting battles against the other.

5

RELIGIONS
The Good, the Bad and the Ugly

○○○

THE HISTORY BIT

One reason why the term 'New Atheists' is applied to figures like Richard Dawkins, Christopher Hitchens, Sam Harris, Daniel Dennett and others is that their endorsement of atheism goes hand in hand with an extremely strong vilification of religion in a way that seems to transcend what has typically been the case. In particular, it is suggested that religion is not just misguided or wrong but actually positively dangerous if not downright malignant. Is religion the source of all the wars, persecution and discrimination we find in the world today? Has it always held back science, reason and learning? Is it like a cancer in humanity that needs to be rooted out entirely? Or is it, as Dawkins suggests, some form of meme that is like a parasite infecting the mind – an idea given short shrift by anthropologists and many other scholars of culture and society as the concept of a 'meme' seems to fulfil no useful function nor have any evidence.

Is religion harmful?

If we seek to answer the question that heads this section, we could consider many issues. Some of these issues, like debates between science and religion or discrimination of women, are dealt with in other chapters. Another issue is whether we are talking about specific religious traditions or the institutions, or even – somehow – the entire range of religions and the inclination to religion of any kind. Furthermore, we may need to ask whether we will think about this across the history of religion or do we mean specifically in the present day. Certainly, critics of religion often take aim at one or the other of them, or differentiate between them. Harris, for instance, seems disparaging towards Islam as a whole, but sees elements of Buddhism (if stripped of what he sees as its more supernatural elements) as positive. Dawkins, while often taking aim at religion as a whole, specifically in his critiques uses Christian and Islamic examples but has also described himself as a 'cultural Anglican' expressing an appreciation of the music and aesthetics. A recent contributor to the debates, Jerry Coyne, sees all 'faith' as harmful, meaning all religion and any world view not based in science (as he understands it). Trying to cover all aspects of the possible debate in this chapter would simply be impossible; therefore, I will make some strategic interventions into particular claims and issues, especially those often raised or that are very contentious, as well as to provide some balance. I will then suggest some ways to move the discussion forward.

I begin with a bit of a conceptual clarification around a few issues. First, talking about religion as some general and universal phenomenon is very difficult (see Chapter 1). Each religion contains very different conceptions about how people should live, what type of deity or transcendent reality exists (see Chapter 4) or what forms of organization they have practised and how this affects society. As such, a very general account of religion as a whole seems problematic. Second, we need to consider that the often used term 'religious people' is also very problematic. In day-to-day life and in terms of their IQ, capacity for love or empathy, or whatever other criteria we choose, we don't find different types of people in religion from anywhere else (just as we shouldn't see all atheists as being some specific group of a certain type of people). As such, some of the very strong rhetoric which suggests that religious people may be part of the problem seems very dangerous and unfounded. This doesn't mean that we can't make any generalizations, but we need to be careful not to make careless, sweeping statements. Third, if we wish to argue that religion is a greater evil than a greater good, we would need to establish some criteria. For instance, how do we weigh or assess the contribution of various religions to the contribution of much of the world's culture, music, art, literature and architecture against harms done through wars, persecutions and oppression in which it may be involved? We should keep these points in mind as we proceed.

I will address three main areas. The first one is the huge field of religious violence, which we will look at from a variety of angles. The second area is a very specific debate which asks whether the world's single largest religious tradition/institution, the Roman Catholic Church, can be said to be a force for good or evil in the world. Finally, I will say something about slavery and human rights.

Religious violence

It is often claimed that religion is responsible for most wars and persecution, and has been responsible, therefore, for more deaths than anything else. This is seen to be exemplified in things like current-day conflicts in the Middle East, for instance, between Israel and Palestine, or in places like Syria, Afghanistan and Iraq. Moreover, historically, we can look to the so-called Wars of Religion that tore through Europe in the sixteenth and seventeenth centuries, the Crusades, the Inquisition or many other examples. The well-known counterargument is that these wars were not about religion but that they were simply political in some way and that religion was used as a justification. It is also pointed out that much of the devastation of the twentieth century was not caused in the name of religion but by various secular or even materialist/atheist ideologies like nationalism and Marxism, as we see with the First and Second World Wars and Stalin's and Mao's purges in the Soviet Union and China, respectively. Behind these two standpoints are often utterly conflicting perceptions of the very nature of religion (of which, as I have mentioned, we should be suspicious): religion is inherently violent and oppressive; religion is inherently peaceful and loving. We will start by setting out some issues.

I begin with what have been called 'texts of terror'. Anyone reading the Christian Old Testament will be struck by the fact that the deity presented in it can be violent and aggressive. That God can seem psychopathic: genocide is justified; the slaughter of enemies down to the last women and children is endorsed and praised; and there are clear injunctions to fight the enemy. Likewise, the Qur'an contains verses which tell its readers to kill – even wipe out – the enemy, and to some this may suggest that it sees war as a good in and of itself. The atheist critic, as indeed critics from other religions, emphasize these verses as proof of the nature of these religions. The conclusion: Christianity, Islam and Judaism are inherently violent and their texts and God endorse war, even by brutal methods. If we stopped here, however, we would have only half the story. The very same texts also tell us to love humanity, endorse tolerance and peace towards other people and also often place violence within a specific context – whether that be self-defence or some specific event. As such, irenic advocates within each religion, and their supporters, use these directives as evidence. The conclusion: Christianity, Islam and Judaism are inherently peaceful and seek always to promote love and tolerance over warfare and hatred.

I would point out something about both approaches, as they tend to use a method very common amongst fundamentalist adherents in different religions: proof-texting, that is, you take a particular passage or verse and use that, and that alone, to show that your point of view is correct. Importantly, this is not just something done by religious advocates. Atheist critics also take individual quotes, often out of context, to enhance their position. This occurs both from religious and non-religious sources. Indeed, humans often seem to like nice, easy-to-use quotes that support what they say. Against this, more thoughtful interpreters within the religion, as well as scholars outside the religions, say we need to understand such things as the message of the text as a whole, how it has been used and interpreted and also the context in which it is written and read. To take one example, Muslims who promote a positive and peaceful interpretation of their religion will point out that the passages which speak about war, violence and killing are far outweighed by passages which talk about other issues, including those which endorse merciful and peaceful attitudes. They will also point out that many of the passages critics often cite are selectively proof-texted, one such being the famous so-called sword verse from the Qur'an (see Box 5.1). However, the whole context of the verses gives a somewhat different meaning than the generally cited and carefully chosen out-of-context phrase. Moreover, Muslims have long held that various verses should be read in the light of others, and as such, for Muslims who understand their religion as one of peace, these verses may be seen as speaking about a particular context in Muhammad's time and what was done then. Other verses which speak of harmony and unity, therefore may be seen to take precedence, for example, this extract: 'So vie one with another in good works. Unto Allah ye will all return…' (Q 5.48).

Box 5.1

The Sword Verse

The infamous sword verse, which is often quoted by critics of Islam goes like this:

> And when the sacred months have passed, then kill the polytheists wherever you find them and capture them and besiege them and sit in wait for them at every place of ambush. But if they should repent, establish prayer, and give zakat, let them [go] on their way. Indeed, Allah is Forgiving and Merciful. (Q 9.5)

Generally, critics will only cite the first part of this verse, and on its own it seems to legitimate indiscriminate killing or offensive warfare. The second part, though, gives another reading, and three points need to be made:

- The idea that it may justify warfare until people convert is directly against another verse in the Qur'an which says there shall be no compulsion in religion (Q 2.256), and Muslim scholars have debated over this.

- While it has been used to justify aggressive warfare and conversion by the sword, it has also been used to argue that one should only fight if there is aggression taking place against Muslims, which leads us to the next point which contextualizes this.

- Originally it seems that it was referring to specific groups with whom there was hostility. As such, the question is: Does it refer to all 'pagans' or only those who were being fought against at that time? Certainly many scholars would say the former, and a principle of traditional Muslim scholarship is that you should know the original context of a verse to correctly interpret it; you cannot just take free-standing passages and use them as you wish. Therefore, the fact that this is understood as a verse dictated in a conflict situation is seen as important. War is already underway, rather than it being an injunction to start aggression. In addition, the final line about God being 'Forgiving and Merciful' can also be read as a context in which these verses should be read (indeed, throughout the whole Qur'an, the most common descriptions of God are as merciful and benevolent), which is seen to indicate that the normal prescription is against warfare.

Another term in Islam that is also often used by critics of Islam is 'jihad', often incorrectly translated into English as 'holy war'. For many Muslims throughout the centuries, jihad has not even primarily been about war, fighting or violence. A famous saying (*hadith*) of Muhammad is that once the wars to establish the tradition in Islam's spiritual home, Mecca, are over, Muslims should move from what he called the 'lesser jihad' (warfare) to the 'greater jihad' (spiritual and moral character building). Paying attention to this would lead us away from seeing jihad principally, or even mainly, as 'warfare'. Despite many critics alleging that jihad as used means 'warfare', it has an equally established, if not more prevalent, usage in Islamic history as personal spiritual perfection. Literally, it simply means 'struggle', and certainly for many Muslims (as for any other group) the primary struggle is with one's own moral character and establishing virtue.

We see that either category of religion as all good or all bad is simply very selective in the way it looks at texts, traditions or facts. Indeed, the scholar Scott Appleby speaks about this as the 'ambivalence of the sacred', or it concerns what theologian and Buddhist scholar Perry Schmidt-Leukel calls the 'oil' and 'water' aspects of religion – it can both stoke the flames of violence and conflict as well as provide resources to put them out!

I will offer here a reading of attitudes towards war and peace within Christianity as an example of how it is hard to say that religions either veer to one side or the other. We must avoid a monolithic reading of 'Christianity' as a single thing. I cannot cover the whole tradition here and focus on what has become the globally dominant form of the tradition, such mainline strands that formed European Christianity; if we considered the Nestorian Church in Asia, we would see a very different dynamic. We begin, as we must, with Jesus. As discussed in Chapters 2 and 3, we need to recall that we're dealing with texts which were created and edited over time; nevertheless, it is possible to get back to some sense of what Jesus may have thought. Some portray him as a pacifist: the meek and mild Jesus. One example is Jesus ordering Peter to stop when he cuts off the ear of the Chief Priest's servant (Matthew 26.15, John 18.10), which is seen as Jesus being against violence. However, I think this interpretation is problematic. If it was a pacifist movement, why was Peter carrying a sword? We know also that earlier in the Gospels, Jesus had asked his disciples to buy swords, and when he was told they had two swords, Jesus replied, 'That's enough' (Luke 22.35–38). Some see this as Jesus mocking his disciples – it is like his saying, 'What, we're going to take on the occupying Roman legions with two swords? Come on guys, get real!' There is, though, a different reading. Since the early twentieth century and the work of Albert Schweitzer (1875–1965), it has been realized that the Jesus of the Gospels is actually living in a very different thought world from ours, and in particular, he was deeply embedded in Jewish apocalyptic thought (eschatology in theological terms). Indeed, elsewhere, Jesus indicates that he believes that God can supply armies of angels on his side. As such, we can read the last passage differently: Jesus is not mocking but telling his disciples that their human efforts will be backed up by huge supernatural forces against which even the might of Rome cannot prevail! Of course, not all scholars read it this way, but I would argue that it provides a viable reading. Either way we know that Jesus' gang was armed. Quite possibly, they had swords for protection from robbers, but still, this is clearly not a pacifist group.

The apocalyptic issue means realizing that Jesus had got it wrong. This is uncomfortable for many Christians; however, it makes the best sense of what we see emerging because it is quite clear that Jesus' earliest followers take on the belief in the end times; scholars of Paul show that his earliest letters are deeply influenced by apocalyptic expectations, but as time goes on, his later writings seem to put this off to some future date, even if there is some hope or expectation that it may be imminent. This excursus may seem to sidetrack us from violence, but it is deeply relevant: the early Jesus movement is countercultural. One way this plays out is in pacifism, a stance that lasted for several centuries. Possibly, this was political expediency; the founder was executed as a traitor against Rome, so the Christians had to show they didn't believe in revolution. However, it fitted their countercultural apocalypticism: the future was in God's hands, and it was not for humanity to overcome others by force.

The fourth century, however, saw a game-changer when the Emperor Constantine (272–337 CE) co-opted Christianity to build his new civil service. Scholars have argued that we see a radical change. It can be observed in art, where images of Jesus as a young, poor, generally beardless figure become transformed into an imperial figure, often bearded and clearly part of the ruling class. It also means that Christians can no longer be pacifists as they need to support the imperial machine. Roman soldiers are now welcomed into the ranks of the church, although anyone who kills another human being still needs to repent; therefore, non-violence remains an ideal. Nevertheless, further changes lie ahead. Augustine of Hippo, famous for innovations in theology, was also influential through his conflicts with heretics in North Africa. At first, he advocated purely peaceful means and preaching, but when it was obvious this wasn't working – indeed, what he saw as heresy was even spreading (heresy, of course, being those forms of belief that the tradition that has power categorizes as such) – he came to rationalize why it would be alright to use force. If heretics converted someone, he reasoned, that person would go to hell, so to protect the innocent and leave their path to heaven open, it was better that heretics should die. This became quite normative thinking in many places in the centuries that followed. This was a major shift: killing was no longer always a bad thing but could sometimes be good. The next step came with the Crusades when, to convince and mobilize an army, the Church argued that killing infidels (i.e. Muslims) was actually a service to the Church and God. It was seen as a way to avoid Purgatory (a place of torment developed in early Christian thought and crystallized in medieval Roman Catholic thought where people not yet ready for heaven could be purged for centuries by fires and torments – and hence, not a place you wanted to stay if it could be avoided). Killing therefore became a religiously good act. As time passed, this became normal. In due course, Christian churches would argue that various forms of killing were justified, such as killing foreigners for your nation. Today it is not expected that Christian soldiers need to repent when they kill others, and military chaplains often see it as their role to explain to Christians who have doubts that what they do is for a greater good.

This is not to say that increasing militarization went unchallenged. Various monastic groups saw problems with it, although some were often complicit. Meanwhile, when the Reformation came many Protestants read Jesus as a pacifist teacher of non-violence. Often persecuted by the mainstream Protestants, who generally taught that rulers needed to maintain order (to put it nicely!), many of these groups were killed, but they continue today in groups like the Quakers, Mennonites and Amish, who often extol pacifism.

To ask if Christianity is a religion of peace requires asking questions: which form of Christianity do we mean; which period exemplifies it; how we interpret the scriptural texts; and what personal stance we hold? Indeed, many prominent campaigns against war, especially against nuclear weapons, as well as arguments for pacifism have come from within religious traditions whether this be Christianity, Islam, Hinduism, Buddhism or others.

The above example of Christianity suggests something that scholars increasingly realize: that the idea that religion, or any particular religion, is inherently peaceful or violent is too simplistic. It employs an essentialist position (where you argue there is an 'essence' of religion) whereby one chosen example, period or reading of a tradition is understood as the norm. Indeed, while religion is often a cause of quite bitter disputes between people, it is fair to say that the answer as to why religious people go to war, or religion is invoked for violent purposes, is basically summed up by one word: politics. This is not to exonerate religion, as it clearly has provided legitimacy for violence and warfare. Would we therefore be better off without religion? Would there be fewer wars if there was no religion? Is religion inherently dangerous (because even if it can provide resources for peace, it can also be used to justify and promulgate war)? Any answer we give would be very speculative, as we simply don't know, as it has never been tried; however, this does not stop us from suggesting an answer.

It has often been stated that the twentieth century disproved that religion was the most dangerous force on the planet, because the major wars and persecutions were fought for other purposes. This was very often nationalism, imperialism or Marxism. Secular, and even avowedly anti-theist regimes and ideologies, have shown that they can inspire people to kill (see Box 5.2).

Box 5.2

> *Does it take religion to make good people do evil things?*
> A much-quoted criticism is Steven Weinberg's one-liner: 'With or without religion, you would have good people doing good things and evil people doing evil things. But for good people to do evil things, that takes religion'. However, it is unclear where such critics base the evidence for this. It is not simply religion that can cause this (indeed, do we really believe there are simply 'all good' or 'all evil' people or deeds?). Hannah Arendt (1906–1975) summed it up in a famous phrase in response to observing some of those who had carried out the Holocaust: 'the banality of evil'. We expect such people to be demonic in some way, but what was found was ordinary-looking people, with ordinary interests, who had been caught up in a world view that led them to do things we see as deplorable. When we look at what people did in places like Pol Pot's (1925–1998) Cambodia, or in the name of particular ideologies, especially nationalism, in the twentieth century, we regrettably see that we do not need religion to persuade ordinary (i.e. good) people to do terrible things.

Meanwhile, religion has also tempered violence. In both medieval Islam and Christianity what is known as a doctrine of the just war developed. Thinkers such as Thomas Aquinas on the Christian side sought to set limits on when wars could be fought. Meanwhile, in Islam, very clear strictures were laid down for the conduct of war: you could not kill women or children (unless attacked by them and therefore defending yourself); likewise Rabbis, priests and monastics were to be unharmed; neither could you seek to destroy the livelihood of your opponents, so farmland would not be burnt, nor shops destroyed and so forth. This latter stricture explains, in part, why many Muslims around the world today cannot reconcile the acts of terrorists and suicide bombers, nor the atrocities committed by the group known as ISIS/Daesh, with their religion. Almost everything that is done in such instances, and in other examples that could be found, go against the way that religion has understood itself, its laws and the conduct it allows. As has been shown by numerous commentators, the violence we see today in the Middle East is led by politics; we see unstable and divided countries, often left in poor condition by imperial control (much of it by Britain and other European nations), being further complicated by the contemporary foreign policies of many Western nations who have supported corrupt dictators, opposed democratic reform and funded militant groups. However, for many political analysts and journalists in the USA, and the West in general, it is far easier and comfortable to tell a simple story about Islam being the problem – fuelled by often semi-knowledgeable ideologues and Islamophobes who find such easy answers conducive to their viewpoints – rather than consider the West's complicity in contemporary terrorism. To point to just one instance, the Mujahadin in Afghanistan were originally funded by the government of the USA to fight against the Soviet Union after the latter invaded. When the Soviet forces left and American funding didn't help create a new state, the Taliban emerged from those groups trained and founded by the USA to fill the political vacuum. As such, funding by the USA, training and failure to ensure political stability once their immediate enemy was defeated is what led to the rise of an extremist threat in that country, something unacknowledged when the USA-led coalition themselves invaded that country and sought to remove this enemy. There clearly is a problem with the type of Islam propagated by the Taliban, ISIS/Daesh, al-Qaeda and other radical groups (as mentioned much of what these types of groups do is not recognized as Islam by many other Muslims), and this needs to be tackled. However, to blame such extremism on Islam *per se* is to ignore a tradition that has inspired peaceful and tolerant people. Indeed, studies consistently show that Islam is not a key factor in radicalization – the recruits of Islamic-linked terrorist organizations often avoid mosques and have little to no religious training or knowledge – but is linked to politics and ideologies (see Box 5.3).

Box 5.3

Black and white

Interesting new research on religious extremism and radicalism suggests one reason why people can be led to bomb and kill innocent civilians, including young children, is a world view that sees no shades of grey: there is simply truth or falsehood – black or white. Some shifts required to enter into such a frame of mind have been studied; however, it is notable that this research, which looks both at world views and also at neuroscience, shows that the vast majority of people tend to think in such dichotomous terms. Humans are naturally inclined to seeing truth and falsehood (i.e. black-and-white thinking). Seeing another's point of view and empathy is hard work. Research has also shown that amongst radical terrorist groups, engineers are vastly over-represented (al-Qaeda's leadership was particularly notable for this). Indeed, it can be argued that fields such as engineering and other science-based disciplines tend to develop black-and-white, right-or-wrong thinking, whereas an education in the humanities looks at interpretation, grey areas and multiple points of view. Indeed, linked to research which shows that many radicals have little to no religious background, one implication is that so-called religious terrorism in not about religion but forms of education that encourage blinkered and narrow attitudes towards whether things are right or wrong, true or false, and gives no other options. Of course, certain religious world views, such as certain trends within Wahhabism (a strictly orthodox Sunni Muslim sect), which is linked to today's Muslim terrorist groups, are also a problem, but this is partly because they, too, promote a monochrome, black-and-white, true-or-false picture of the world. Equally, we tend to need certain forms of political and social factors as a catalyst; for example, extremism is not one-dimensional, but empathy for those different from ourselves seems to delimit it. But the same thinking underlies so-called religious violence, right-wing extremism and all other forms of violent militancy. When atheists vilify religion as uniquely bad, or suggest that it is a cancer, we are seeing the creation of narratives that can justify such violence.

It is noteworthy that while Christianity and Islam are often cited as the examples of violent religions, Hinduism and Buddhism have often been understood as peaceful – an understanding promoted by many within these religions. Violence, however, occurs in these world views too, as exemplified by contemporary Hindu nationalist militants in India, and the war-like rhetoric coming from places like Sri Lanka, Myanmar and Thailand. This is despite the fact that the central Buddhist scriptures contain no divine endorsements to warfare. Indeed, they are explicit that the killing of any sentient (feeling) being is wrong. However, nationalist narratives make an association between Buddhism and national identity, justifying violence. For instance, many Sri Lankans see their nation as the homeland of 'true' Buddhism and, as such, defending Sri Lanka and defending Buddhism becomes synonymous for many. This acts as a reminder that all world views, not simply religious ones, are open to abuse.

Is the Catholic Church a force for good in the world?

The next question we will address is whether the Catholic Church is a force for good in the world today. I choose this topic partly because it is the single largest religious organization in the world and, as such, carries incredible influence. However, I also choose it because there was a very interesting debate held by Intelligence Squared (a debate platform) in which the British comedian and atheist Stephen Fry and the late Christopher Hitchens (a New Atheist) argued that it was not, while the British politician Anne Widdecombe and the African Archbishop Onaiyekan argued that it was. Starting off with a relatively even vote between the two sides, but with a large undecided number to target in the debate (the motion: 'The Catholic Church is a force for good in the world'; initial votes – for: 678; against: 1102; don't know: 346), it ended with a vote that can only be described as the religious side being humiliated, that is, not just having the balance of undecided tipping against them but also losing a large number of their original supporters (votes afterwards – for: 268; against: 1876; don't know: 34).

It is not my intention to salvage the Church's reputation from this debacle, although it must be said that both the atheist speakers were excellent rhetoricians, while the Catholic advocates were not (the Archbishop, in particular, obviously speaking in a way that I am sure would be convincing in his homeland, but I think was very unappealing to the kind of Western middle-class audience that attended this event). As such, what it showed was mainly the quality of the panel. Nevertheless, the Catholic Church is clearly a deeply problematic institution. Its stance on contraception is clearly a public health disaster and has been responsible for the spread of AIDS/ HIV, as well as being unconducive to women's health and population control (although a softening of this stance may have been hinted at by Pope Francis). It has persecuted and oppressed many for what it deems doctrinal deviance, or simply for challenging its authority. Also, child abuse scandals have rocked it internationally. In fact, its protection of child abusers in its ranks is little different from the way that, for instance, senior British politicians and public figures, including major celebrities, were offered refuge by major public institutions and colleagues. Arguably, though, that this happened within a religious institution is a greater sign of hypocrisy. It did not, however, act the way it did because it was a religious organization – it acted to protect its reputation and members the way (unfortunately) that any large institution tends to act. Despite the awful things that have happened within it and under its auspices, this is not the whole picture. Throughout the world, the Catholic Church sends out missionaries and monastics who run hospitals, schools and other services. While Mother Teresa (1910–1997) was a controversial case, if the Catholic health and educational institutions around the world were closed, the provision of these services in many countries would be devastated. Even in developed Western countries many notable schools, universities and hospitals still continue to be led, funded or staffed by the Catholic Church. I do not wish to argue that this outweighs the harm the institution has done; rather, I wish to point out that from a more distanced standpoint we cannot simply say that it is a force for good or evil in the world. Certainly, I would also suggest that the vote which took place while the rather hard-line Pope Benedict XVI was in command, was a time when the Church was perhaps not receiving good press. Perhaps the more media-friendly Pope Francis, with an encyclical on climate change, which has even received positive comment from those who are typically critics of religion like scientist Neil deGrasse Tyson, may see a different sentiment persist. Francis' outspoken comments on the exploitation of the poor have also won him many admirers (and critics). I raise this, though, to show that to some degree, the perception of a huge institution like the Catholic Church rests upon a range of factors. I believe it fair to say that Catholicism is better thought of under Pope

Francis than it was under Pope Benedict XVI; at least it receives more favourable media coverage. But does this mean it is now a force for good, whereas it wasn't before? As noted, we sometimes ask questions which are far too simplistic. Without the Catholic Church, we would not have many schools, universities and hospitals, including many of the world's best. This, of course, does not prove it is a force for good rather than otherwise, but points to the way that religious institutions are woven into the very fabric of our societies, such that simply asking such questions misses a lot of the history, activity and nature of what a 'religion' may be.

Slavery and human rights

We come now to consider a range of issues relating to human rights where advocates of religion or atheist sceptics have disagreed. I will not suggest that we should be on one side or the other; rather, I will seek to show that the discourse is generally very problematic, if not downright distorted.

We begin with slavery. As atheist critics point out, texts like the Bible and Qur'an provide justification for slavery and taking slaves, a normal practice in their times. Even if we allow, as I believe the historical record suggests we need to allow, that the abolition of slavery was actually significantly empowered by evangelical Christians who understood their faith as requiring that all be treated and regarded as equal, the atheist critique remains on two counts: First, how can we base our ethics on books which not just assume such things, but even endorse them. We have moved on ethically and this simply shows that the ethical values are suited, at best, to another age. Second, even if religious people now oppose slavery, religion contains the potential to advocate for things such as slavery, which go against human rights and contemporary values. Nevertheless, I would suggest that this is problematic for a couple of reasons. One of them is that Christianity was actually at the forefront of the campaign to end slavery, as it actually supplied the basis upon which we now come to understand slavery as wrong. While Christianity may not have been the only source of such ideas and may not be necessary today to supply them, the counterargument assumes that it is inherently dangerous (see below). It also assumes that what is written in texts supplies the essence of what a religion is. As we have discussed, people do not read any books in this way; rather, they are always interpreted (see Chapter 2). In a world where religion remains a strong force, it is arguably best to advocate positive readings rather than simply denigrating the books and those who read them.

This brings me to a particular example. Throughout human history many (all?) cultures have divided the world into 'us' and 'them'; for the Greeks and Chinese this was between the civilized (us) and the barbarians (them). Anyone who has watched the film *The Missionary* will be aware that such ways of thinking resulted in the attitude that certain groups of people were inherently inferior to others, such that they could be enslaved. What the film (based on historical examples) shows, in the South American context, is the way that the main advocates against this commodification of the other, essentially with secular powers using them for gain and benefit, was the Church. It was a religious claim that all people were equal that opposed this. Again, in the nineteenth century, as European empires expanded, a secular rationalist and scientific discourse sought to divide people into categories, with white Europeans as the highest and then through various other grades. Again, it was Christians, principally evangelical Christians, who were at the forefront of opposing this kind of viewpoint. Quite clearly, as science has developed, it has recognized the very faulty discourses that were shaping what were essentially racist attitudes, which chose certain features of particular races as signs of their superiority. Nevertheless, in these contexts, relatively recent in human history, it was religion's rationality, arguing from purely theological resources, that opposed secular and instrumental rationality, and was found to be supporting the best ethical principles. I assume most atheists today will agree with religious people on this: all humans are equal and need to be treated as such. Of course, religion was also used to justify the apartheid regimes in South Africa and was used in the southern USA as an ideology for the Ku Klux Klan and other racist groups, notwithstanding that this is quite difficult to defend and never found much favour more generally. Of course, the opponents of such regimes also invoked religion. Nevertheless, the principle that all humans should all be treated equally is arguably an impulse that has arisen in history as a religious impulse against secular powers which wish to argue otherwise. I would therefore suggest that to see religion as always stuck in archaic texts and periods and so never equal to rational and secular ethics is problematic. We need to realize that, to a large extent, whether we see religion or atheism as morally superior or inferior is highly contextual. What issues do we highlight? Which battles are being fought? Which side has influenced the other?

I turn to one last example of a dispute: attitudes to homosexuality. While there have been Christian arguments for equality, it is fair to say that in many parts of the world opposition to homosexuality is based on religious arguments (although how far this represents cultural prejudice rather than scripture is debatable; see Box 5.4). This seems to be the case in much of the southern USA, where opposition to the 2015 Supreme Court ruling that same-sex marriage should be legal everywhere across the nation has been opposed by those using primarily Christian biblical passages and examples to oppose it. Similar things can be found globally. In terms of its ability to adapt to current human rights standards, religion seems lacking. However, certain statistics show something different. In a number of surveys across the UK it has been shown that opposition to homosexuality in general, including same-sex marriage, is higher amongst those who identify as religious. However, when broken down demographically, something interesting happens. In almost all age ranges the opposition is far higher amongst the religiously affiliated; however, amongst those under 25 years of age it has been found that those who claim a religious identity are actually more in favour of same-sex marriage and oppose homophobia more than their non-religious peers. Now this may be a statistical anomaly or a blip, but it has occurred across a number of surveys by various polling groups and suggests something I have suggested at various places in this book, that is, religion cannot be treated as saying one thing, or believing one thing. Indeed, in at least one demographic, the religious lead the atheists in their attitude on progressive moral issues.

I would like to tentatively propose a hypothesis: just as it was an understanding that the biblical message was first and foremost about equality, which saw Christians leading the two debates we mentioned above, so perhaps religious believers, especially amongst the younger generation, may come to be leaders on a global scale when it comes to such contemporary social and ethical changes and expectations, such as an acceptance of homosexuality. This is very speculative, but it is notable that across the USA a number of high-profile evangelical Christian leaders have, over recent years, crossed the battle lines on this debate and decided that they interpret the Bible to mean that we should accept homosexuality and same-sex marriage. (Perhaps it is worth saying that one can only hope.)

Box 5.4

Does the Bible condemn homosexuality?

Most Christians who oppose same-sex marriage, or homosexuality as a way of life or practice, say that their reasons lie within the Bible. Quite a few passages are quoted as examples, for instance Leviticus 18.22 and 20.13, the story of Lot, Sodom and Gomorrah (Genesis 19), 1 Corinthians 6.9–11 and 1 Timothy 1.8–11. However, as biblical scholars have pointed out, we do not see aversion to homosexuality as it is understood today. First, Leviticus 18.22 is part of what is often termed the Purity Code, a set of laws for priests before they entered the Jerusalem Temple and involved the necessity to purify oneself before ritual. The language that it is 'deplorable' or 'an abomination' needs to be read in this context, where other things that were also condemned included certain shellfish products, wearing mixed-fabric garments, having tattoos and other things, which Christians have decided do not apply to them. The story of Lot, meanwhile, is actually a condemnation of a lack of hospitality, which is a key biblical virtue. The issue of male rape also has to be put alongside Lot's apparent willingness to let his daughters be raped, if we want to take moral lessons from this story. The passages from the New Testament, meanwhile, are amongst general lists of transgressions, which include things like gossip. Are all gossipers to be condemned to hell for their behaviour? Moreover, technical terms are used – 'catamite' and 'sodomite' – which refer, in the Roman social context, to the practice of an older man and a younger male slave or prostitute. As such, it can be seen as a condemnation of iniquitous exploitation or abuse. Nowhere is a consensual and loving relationship between two partners mentioned. Leviticus 20.13 may seem more problematic as it involves a death penalty; however, it goes alongside this penalty being allotted for other transgressions such as cursing one's mother and father, as well as adultery. These punishments, again, are things Christians no longer see as permissible. As such, for Christians to pick out homosexuality as uniquely stigmatized as a 'sin' in the Bible is to interpret the text in a way that ignores the way they otherwise use this text, or to fail to ask what is actually condemned.

THINKING ABOUT RELIGIONS TODAY

The horror inflicted upon people in the name of religion has been one of the primary reasons for many people to leave religions and embrace atheism, and every religious tradition and organization needs to look at their record. Indeed, Dennett once remarked that 'You don't get to advertise all the good that your religion does without first scrupulously subtracting all the harm it does and considering seriously the question of whether some other religion, or no religion at all, does better'. We have addressed the question of the Catholic Church above. Of course, one flip side of this would be that no atheist should criticize the bad things any religion does without scrupulously considering all the good it has done, lofty ideals it has inspired, cultural achievements to which it has given birth and moral progress it has encouraged, and consider also whether any religion or world view has done better or worse. Another flip side is that before any religion criticizes atheism, atheists or secularism, it needs to consider the good and noble ideas which have come from this source too, and the benefits which have come to humanity from those holding such views. It is really hard to know how to do this. How do we weigh the benefits of founding the European university system against restricting education in other contexts? Do we look at the lives of every individual inspired or simple proclamations of deeds by specific institutions? What would count as Christianity would depend on which institutions we included within this. Certainly, many believers (a claim made by significant Christian movements since at least the time of Constantine) would argue that the more formal hierarchy of the churches are corrupt and do not really represent their faith! Indeed, any attempt to count the good or bad done by religion, or atheism, would probably tell us far more about the person doing the assessment than that tradition itself: what is emphasized, which bits of the tradition, what actually counts as 'religious' and what doesn't, and so forth.

In the contemporary period, though, one standard which all should agree on is freedom of religion and belief, including, of course, the freedom not to hold *any* religion. This is built into the Universal Declaration of Human Rights brought into being by the United Nations in 1948. Indeed, complete freedom is generally seen as one of the signs of the modern secular state, instituted with the Enlightenment. This followed the so-called Wars of Religion, which wracked Europe for several hundred years and was seen as needing a new basis for religious tolerance. Notwithstanding that the popular perception of these as Catholic–Protestant wars fought for religion has no historical validity; the wars concerned the creation of modern nation states, and it can be shown that Catholics fought Catholics, and Catholics and Protestants fought other Catholic and Protestants, while Protestants fought Protestants as much as, if not more than, Catholics and Protestants ever made discrete sides (which, even when they did, tended to represent specific national opponents rather than denominational opponents). Indeed, when the Enlightenment thinkers sought a model of religious freedom they looked not to secular ideals but to the Muslim Ottoman Empire, which included many religious groupings but saw no religious battle lines. Historically, it was therefore Islam which provided the model for the religious freedom that underlies our modern secular state, with figures like John Locke (1632–1704) writing admiringly of their system. Of course, the Islamic ideal is far from perfect from our contemporary standpoint. The *millet* system of the Ottomans provided military levies from non-Muslim communities. This built on Islamic precedent such as the Medina Constitution and the Pact of Umar, which provided protection for other religions and the right to worship as they wished and run their own affairs as 'People of the Book' (originally Jews, Christians and a mysterious group called Sabeans, but later as Islamic Empires grew, this recognition was extended to Hindus, Zoroastrians and Buddhists). In return for a *jizya*, generally translated as 'poll tax', they were exempted from military duty and given protection (so antithetical to the Ottoman Muslim example). Of course, today, we do not expect various religious groups, or those with minority philosophical or political views, to pay a special tax to ensure their protection, although in much mainstream Islamic legal thought the *jizya* was set at the same level as Islamic alms giving (*zakat*) at 2.5% and so acted as an equivalent taxation. Indeed, the stories of persecution of Christians and other minorities witnessed today in various Muslim-majority countries are in complete violation of the Islamic injunctions of how it should treat minorities under its rule. While the Pact of Umar falls short of modern standards, it exceeds much contemporary practice – both the inequitable treatment of Christians and others in some Muslim-majority countries, but also it arguably would not violate basic religious freedoms under international human rights, as some extreme secularisms do. Indeed, starting from the principle that Islam far exceeded the norms and expectations of religious freedom of its day, some contemporary Muslim scholars argue that the past concepts need to be further extended in a greater understanding of Islamic tenets. Critics may say this is impossible, but that denies the sheer facts of history: religions have always changed as societies change (this may be, as some atheists argue, because they are simply human products). However, the Islamic practice of Shariah and jurisprudence (Islamic law and legal interpretation), which is the system under which such judgements would be made, is capable of adaptation. During the Middle Ages some scholars argued that novel interpretation was no longer possible (in technical terms, the gates of *itjihad*, independent thinking, were declared closed), but scholars for the past couple of hundred years have said that new interpretation is legitimate (i.e. the gates of *itjihad* are open). Determining this depends on the Muslim community, but clearly, novel interpretations are arising within the tradition. Some of these interpretations are very negative, and in line with this I would suggest that those outside the Muslim community should support those who argue for more positive ideals. Indeed, the legal opinions (*fatwa* – in most of Islam this term simply denotes a jurist's opinion; it is not binding) that support Muslim terrorism and extremism are often those which most violate the historical principles (both because they are often delivered by people without the requisite knowledge and training, and for contravening established rulings).

We have ended up discussing human rights, something which in general, atheists say are supported by themselves but opposed by religions. However, one important right that is enshrined in international human rights law is freedom of religion and belief, and alongside this is the right to protect and maintain your tradition and, in relation to the rights to family life, for parents to educate their children as they see fit. A number of atheists, most notably Richard Dawkins, have, however, argued that to bring children up within a religious tradition is a form of child abuse, and that children should not be brought up religiously. If we take human rights to be statements of what we as a society collectively believe in and stand for, and we criticize those who don't respect them (a case that Dawkins and others frequently hurl at various religious communities), then we find that at least some atheists must also stand accused on these grounds. Of course, Dawkins and others may say that they don't agree with certain human rights and think they should be changed; however, we then enter another area of debate wherein we ask who decides, and on what grounds, which human rights are the 'good ones' and which are the 'bad ones' (or which apply to us and which don't) – a game that various dictators around the world like playing. Of course, a number of atheists disagree with Dawkins on this matter, and he has been described as a 'fundamentalist' atheist by some people for what seem to be his extreme and sometimes quite vehement views. It is raised, though, to show that all traditions have their differences while they change and evolve. Personally, while I disagree with Dawkins about the right to teach religion to children, I would join him in arguing that parents should not have the right to insist that their children be taught creationism instead of evolution. Some would oppose both Dawkins and myself on this. As always, we need to see the variety: not all atheists are against religion, but some are; not all religious believers are against human rights, but some are; some atheists are against human rights; and some (actually, many) religious believers are in favour of human rights.

6

WOMEN, BODIES AND GENDER

○ ○ ○

THE THEORY BIT

The religious traditions of the world, it has to be said, have a pretty poor track record when it comes to the fair and equal treatment of women. While some Christian churches today have opted for female leadership, the world's largest denomination, the Roman Catholics, maintain a strictly male hierarchy and priesthood. The same holds true across the Orthodox Churches and many others. Across many religions, scriptural and traditional injunctions are used to suggest that women should have a subservient position in relation to men, subject to the dictates of their fathers and husbands, and sometimes they are unable to work or go about other forms of business in ways that many see as indicative of modernity and civilization. At the same time, while not wanting to vindicate the abuses of religion, it must be acknowledged that the world as a whole has fallen short in this area and, even in countries such as the USA, which see themselves as being at the forefront of human rights and representative of progress, women remain disadvantaged in many areas of life. Meanwhile, that area of life often taken by many atheists as the antithesis of religion and the paradigm of progress – science – is itself ridden with sexism and glass ceilings, meaning that it remains dominated by men and operates in ways that often implicitly exclude women. Certainly, it is very different in that no foundational text says it should be this way, but the issue of the oppression of women is far bigger simply than religion.

In this chapter, we will look at a variety of discourses on women across religious traditions, in part showing that the sexism often demonstrated is not universal yet at the same time deeply ingrained. We will also address the question of the way that religion has treated sexuality and the body.

Patriarchy in Christianity

One theory which is posited is that societies were matriarchal until several thousand years ago, and images of fecund female deities appear in the archaeological record, which suggest that worship often centred around a mother goddess. The change to patriarchy, on this theory, is associated with the rise of male sky (it should also be said, I think, mountain) gods, who represented a changing society. At this time, women moved from being revered leaders to subjected second-class citizens as a male agenda was enforced on society. A related argument is that of Friedrich Engels (1820–1895), who suggests that the change arose with the advent of private property in pastoral and agrarian societies, wherein women became part of property; it was noted that hunter-gatherer societies are not polarized into male domination and female submission. The historical evidence for such a thesis is not overwhelming and it remains very much theory. Whatever the case, while in some places matriarchal societies can be found, the overwhelming majority of human societies that we have known, and which still exist, have been patriarchal in nature. It is difficult to know whether religion has simply reflected this in the way that they were set up, or if they were actively complicit in constructing the agenda. Whatever the case, today, various parts of the scripture reflect a time when a male hierarchy was not only the norm but expected. Taking such texts literally today is seen as a problem and means that religions – according to critics both within and without – are inherently patriarchal and sexist. The criticism that has come from within has often been just as harsh as that from without. The American feminist theologian Mary Daly (1928–2010), whose journey took her beyond Christianity, once scathingly remarked: 'If God is male, then the male is God'. Other female theologians, such as Rosemary Radford Ruether, have taken a different reading and suggested that women's traditions can be found and renewed. We will begin by looking at some of the evidence within the religions.

It is often remarked that compared with the society around him, Jesus was remarkably open towards women. The evidence of the Gospels shows that he had female disciples and that he allowed them to listen to his teachings as equals. The story of Mary and Martha is indicative, where Mary complains that Martha is simply sitting listening to Jesus' teachings (like, we presume, the male disciples), while she should be like *her*, at work serving food (Luke 10.38–42). In the context of the times, Jesus' response (that she had chosen the 'better part' by listening) is quite shocking, and we have very little evidence of women being able to receive such teachings elsewhere in his society. Again, scholars have noted the central role of women in his life story – for example, the first sighting of Jesus after his resurrection (whether you believe in this event as a physical event or not is beside the point, as it is the role of women in the story on which we are focusing) was by Mary Magdalene – and women are portrayed in this sense as the first believers, and needing to convince the men. In a strongly patriarchal society, that women are given a role as the first teachers and are the paradigmatic disciples, is quite remarkable. Of course, they soon disappear from the story as it becomes about the male disciples. Nevertheless, there are some clear indications that Jesus regarded women very highly, notably in Luke's Gospel, sometimes called 'the women's Gospel'. This, of course, does not erase the sexism of the later tradition, but it does suggest that Christians who subjugate women are not following Jesus' example.

In the story of how the tradition developed, Saul of Tarsus, generally known as Saint Paul, often takes the role of the villain. For many he is the person who turned a religion about Jesus' teachings into a religion about Jesus and also turned a proto-feminist tradition into a misogynistic and strongly patriarchal one. Anyone who has watched the television series *QI* will be familiar with the idea that everything you think you knew is wrong, and this is certainly an example. It is not the time to go into the how and why of one person apparently turning a tradition around completely, but we *can* deal with the question of women in Paul's writings. One particularly cited passage is 1 Corinthians 14.33b–35. However, structural problems in the text suggest it was not written, as it now stands, by Paul (see Box 6.1). As well as the structural problems with the passage, scholars have also unearthed textual evidence which shows that many of the earliest texts do not include the sexist passage. It appears to first emerge in a text in Asia Minor and then over the next few centuries spreads out to become universal. Meanwhile, in Chapter 2, we discussed the fact that when the Early Church came to collect Paul's letters, scholars today believe that while mostly correct, some texts probably not written by him were included. The reason for this is partly the style and theology, which do not match what Paul says elsewhere, but also other reasons. It emerges from this that another letter, 1 Timothy, which contains another misogynistic passage by 'Paul' is also not by Paul himself. Notably, the fact that it is misogynistic was not used by scholars to consider it as not being genuine, as the normative assumption based on this and the passage cited above, is that Paul was anti-women. Our evidence, though, is not simply negative (that the more problematic verses attributed to him are actually not genuine parts of his writings) for there are some other quite remarkable pieces that suggest that Paul was anything but a misogynist.

Box 6.1

Should women keep silent in church?
Critics of Paul, the Bible and Christianity are familiar with one particular passage which we can quote in full:

> Let two or three prophets speak and let the others weigh what is said. If a revelation is made to another sitting by, let the first be silent. For you can all prophesy one by one, so that all may learn and be encouraged; and the spirits of prophets are subject to prophets. For God is a God of confusion but a God of peace. What! Did the word of God originate with you, or are you the only ones it has reached? If anyone thinks that he is a prophet, or spiritual, he should acknowledge that what I am writing to you is a command of the Lord. If any one does not recognize this, he is not recognized. So, my brethren, earnestly desire to prophesy, and do not forbid speaking in tongues; but all things should be done decently and in order (1 Corinthians 14.29–33a, 36–40).

> Those familiar with this passage (or paying attention to the reference) will note that I haven't actually quoted it in 'full', but what I want you to notice is that what is given here makes sense and appears to be a logical and coherent argument. However, if I had quoted it in full between the sentence ending ' ...but a God of peace' and the one beginning 'What! Did the word of God originate...', the following would have appeared:
>
>> As in all the churches of the saints, the women should keep silence in the churches. For they are not permitted to speak, but should be subordinate as even the law says. If there is anything they desire to know, let them ask their husbands at home. For it is shameful for a woman to speak in church (1 Corinthians 14.33b–35).
>
> Now go back and read the whole passage in full including this section, and what I think you will notice is that the flow of the argument is interrupted and what seems to be an entirely alien idea is suddenly inserted mid-flow. Therefore, scholars argue that this is an insertion and not part of the original text. Ancient manuscripts also show it being absent in most of the earliest versions but appearing in Asia Minor in the second century and gradually becoming the standard text.

One of these passages from Paul seems to us quite innocuous, and if we read it, we would simply pass it by, but it goes like this: 'Greet Prisca and Aquila, my fellow workers in Jesus Christ...' (Romans 16.3). Why is this remarkable? The answer is very simple: the wife's name is put before that of her husband. This was simply not done in the classical world: custom dictated that the male, the husband, should always come first. Indeed, scholars have noted that we only have one other instance from the classical period where the woman's name comes before that of her husband, and this is because that woman was the mother of an emperor. Paul's usage can therefore be considered unique (even if other examples come to light, it would still be striking and remarkable) of giving the woman more honour and prestige than her husband. Clearly this was a man prepared to go against his culture's expected ordering of male and female. Some other passages are also important but very contested. In those passages, Paul includes women amongst the list of disciples and preachers in the

Church (see Philemon and Philippians 4.2–3). The clear implication is that women had equality in the hierarchy as leaders. At this stage the system of bishops, priests, deacons and others had not emerged, so the terminology does not say that women are priests and bishops, and this is why it is contested by traditionalist Christian theologians to say that they never had this role. Such a reading, however, goes against the clear implications of the text and what we know about the way the terminology was used in this period. Indeed, there are indications, and good evidence, that women remained leaders and priests (perhaps even bishops) within the emerging Christian church for several centuries. Either way, Paul clearly gave equality to women within his missionary work, and even (as noted of Priscilla) accorded them honours that are remarkable in the ancient world.

When we come to consider the question of whether Christianity is inherently sexist or opposed to women's leadership, the evidence suggests that the foundational sources accord women full rights as leaders. Of course, I am not saying that the Christian Church is inherently feminist and progressive, we have a history that tells us otherwise. Let's put the issue in these terms, though: Does this suggest that the problem is 'religion' or the surrounding culture? It could be argued that the Jesus movement began (at least in the persons of Jesus as Paul) as a progressive proto-feminist movement but that in the face of the surrounding patriarchal culture, this message was subsumed, lost and eventually overturned. This does not tell us that we need to return to religion; however, it suggests that simplistic caricatures of religion as inherently regressive and always opposed to women are based more on prejudice than an understanding of the historical facts.

Patriarchy in other religions

Daoism is perhaps the religion with the most positive attitude towards women over history. In its best known version, the famous foundational text, the Daodejing (sometimes Tao Te Ching, or known as the Lao Zi or Lao Tze after its alleged author) employs the Chinese concept of yin–yang to praise the feminine principle of yin as, if anything, superior. This valuing of the yin and its spiritual qualities has meant that sometimes women have been seen as more capable, or inherently advantaged, in developing their spiritual life. Historically, the Quan

Zhen Dao tradition (one of two main Daoist schools which still exist today) also had female lineages, which were entirely self-maintained and not subject to male jurisdiction. This no longer continues, as the past few hundred years have seen them all subsumed as subsets of male lineages, partly because the idea of such female autonomy ran contrary to Chinese cultural norms. Both Christian and Buddhist monastic lineages have always prioritized the male as superior: Buddhist nuns have been answerable to their male compatriots; Christian nuns need a male priest for their spiritual oversight. This is not to say, though, that there have not been very powerful and significant female leaders in all traditions at different times.

The Islamic tradition is an interesting case to consider and one often subject to criticism today. The interest comes from the fact that, for its day, Islam saw women given far more rights and privileges as well as protections than they had in Arab society at the time; given that before they had virtually none this may not be difficult, critics could suggest. Nevertheless, they had rights which, in certain ways, exceeded those of women in Europe until at least the nineteenth century. Certainly though, the rights of women in nineteenth-century Europe, or traditional Muslim countries, often fall far short of what are considered to be normative rights today. The question is therefore raised: Does Islam have a progressive attitude towards women that seeks to move them beyond the situation society gave them – something as applicable in seventh-century Arabia as it is today – or is it stuck in a seventh-century Arabian context? Some critics would suggest that if the religion changes from the original prescriptions, then it shows that the presupposed divine rules are not suitable for contemporary society and therefore the whole system should be discarded. This, however, offers a very simplistic reading of what religions actually say and do, and that while some exponents of them would agree (it is a take-it-or-leave-it complete package which cannot be changed), it is not the way that religions have tended to understand themselves. Indeed, Islam understands the term Shariah, its legal system, to relate to its root-word meaning 'a path (through the desert)', which could indicate that it is not a once-and-for-all given system, but rather a journey that people need to work out as they go along. Indeed, a desert path may lead to an oasis. Advancing stereotypes or simplistic caricatures does not lead to helpful discussions. (For a discussion on the relationship of Islamic texts and cultural practices on divorce, marriage and honour, see Box 6.2.)

We can note some key points about the early Islamic tradition as well as what occurs today. First, it needs to be stated that one verse often seen as problematic is the following:

> Men are in charge of women by [right of] what Allah has given one over the other and what they spend [for maintenance] from their wealth. So righteous women are devoutly obedient, guarding in [the husband's] absence what Allah would have them guard. But those [wives] from whom you fear arrogance – [first] advise them; [then if they persist], forsake them in bed; and [finally], strike them. But if they obey you [once more], seek no means against them. Indeed, Allah is ever Exalted and Grand (Q 4.34).

This clearly sets out a hierarchy, which some Islamic traditionalists have used to suggest women should always be subject to men. Islamic tradition, however, gives examples like Khadija, Muhammad's first wife, who was clearly a successful business woman in her own right and so had a public role. While the most prominent of Muhammad's later wives, Aisha, who had a prominent role both spiritually – many *hadith* or sayings of Muhammad were authenticated by her – and politically, leading a faction into war in what was known as the Battle of the Camel; that she lost, has however, been cited by some as evidence that women should not have political leadership. The Qur'an, though, highlights the Queen of Sheba who rules successfully, in part due to her feminine qualities. Islamic societies have also historically seen some examples of female leadership, while today it is notable that a good number of Muslim-majority countries, including Bangladesh, Indonesia, Pakistan and Turkey, have produced a succession of high-profile female leaders (prime ministers or presidents), a feat not equalled by many Western secular democracies.

Box 6.2

Divorce, marriage and honour in Islam

Women's rights in areas like marriage and divorce are also subject to criticism, but as the Canadian scholar, Lynda Clarke, has argued, much of what goes on in practice is actually contrary to qur'anic injunctions and introduced in opposition to Shariah principles. The Qur'an, for instance, states both that divorce is an abomination and that any man wishing to divorce his wife must have a waiting period before setting her aside. The practice of instant divorces is a blatant violation of this, and as Clarke shows, was brought into Islamic law simply as a recognition that people were doing this but against the arguments of Islamic jurists and the Qur'an itself. It therefore simply attempted to regulate what it saw as an abuse. Likewise, Islamic tradition is very clear that no woman should be forced to marry against her will, while she is provided with a dower as her own inviolate property on marriage so that she has financial independence. In practice, however, in many countries arranged marriages and control of this money is done against such traditions. Likewise, honour killings seem to be a pre-Islamic custom, that Clarke again shows the Qur'an and early Islamic tradition sought to stamp out but which has remained strong in various tribal contexts.

Veiling is another contested arena; however, Islamic feminist scholars have pointed out that the Qur'an does not imply this, rather saying that women should cover their bosom. Calls for modesty in dress apply to both men and women. That attitudes towards appropriate head coverings vary so widely across the Islamic world is some indication that these are very much local traditions and are not in any sense inherent to Islam. Indeed, the tradition that Muhammad's wives were veiled seems to reflect influences from the nearby Christian Byzantine Empire, where this practice was common amongst noble and high-class women so they would be 'protected' from the gaze of the lower classes. The practice is therefore far more class based than religious in origins.

The veiling of Muhammad's wives (if they even were veiled, as it is far from clear historically that this was the case) was a sign of high-class status. Of course, today, many Muslim women choose to veil as a sign of their devotion. It is also seen as a mark of a rejection of the way that (Western) capitalist consumer society makes women commodities for the male gaze in the kind of clothing and fashions that predominate in the market. Indeed, the move towards covering the hair in places like Turkey and other Muslim-majority countries is often strong amongst educated middle-class women for precisely the reason that they do not wish to be judged by their looks and outward physical appearance. Feminists from the West have for some time come to recognize that exporting a US–European version of what feminism means can be problematic. Certainly, I have sympathies for the rejection of female commoditization that veiling can represent. This, of course, is very different from when women are forced to veil, or otherwise limited within the public sphere. Moreover, the attempts of some white male Western atheists to 'save' Muslim women from Muslim men has been likened by Islamic feminist scholars like Jerusha Lamptey to the kind of colonial discourses that were common in the days of European empires. Indeed, Lamptey has noted as well, the ignorance of saying that Muslim women need to be given feminism, ignores the Islamic feminist movements which already exist globally; rather, Lamptey and others have suggested that what Muslim women would like are allies in their work, not 'crusading saviours' (my phrase, not hers) who may do more harm than good by suggesting that feminist ideas are anti-Islamic and inherently hostile to religion.

This brief survey notes several points. First, blanket caricatures or assertions that women are oppressed across the 'Islamic world' (i.e. in Muslim-majority countries) is simply not true. Muslim-majority countries have had more female elected heads of state than most Western secular democracies. In many countries, there are simply no restrictions. This is not to say that a number of particularly Arab countries, but some elsewhere, do not impose restrictions on women: Saudi Arabia and Afghanistan are prominent examples. In each case the kind of restrictions, on clothing, roles in the public sphere or education (we have not mentioned this, but the example of Muhammad makes it clear that women should be educated, while throughout Islamic history women were taught and became scholars) reflect particular local customs, not anything inherent in the Qur'an or Islamic tradition. While some verses of the Qur'an, notably 4.34, do place women in a disadvantaged situation, and while inheritance laws far exceeded anything of their time, they do not fit modern patterns of equality. This is clearly a problem for many atheists, and something with which many Muslims today are coming to terms. Nevertheless, simply suggesting that Islam has an entirely negative influence both historically and in the contemporary context is inaccurate.

Some suggest that the Hindu family of religions, because of its many goddesses, is more proto-feminist; however, the goddess traditions are dominated by a male priesthood, while the texts and traditions have tended to be written by men and for men. Furthermore, the Laws of Manu (c. second century BCE) clearly stipulates that a woman will be subject to her father before marriage, to her husband during marriage and to her son after her husband passes away. In marriage, indeed, her role is often seen simply to produce a son to carry on the male line. Of course, the implementation of such ideas has not been universal, and in the historical Vedic period (before the sixth century BCE), it seems that women had an equal status as religious teachers and potentially within society at large. Indeed, the idea that the Laws of Manu should provide a guiding narrative for all women in Indian society is very possibly an implementation of British colonial rule. The British sought members of the elite classes to codify and standardize a Hindu law code across the subcontinent. Likewise, the practice of *suttee*, widow burning, prior to British rule seems to have been very limited in geographical practice, simply to a few small areas, and had always been only a practice for the very highest ruling classes and performed in certain historical contexts. With British scholars attempting to find universalized rules which applied across the whole of Hinduism (better spoken of as a variety of different traditions than a single 'religion') this, like many other things, was promoted, partly for propaganda purposes, as a barbaric and universal Hindu tradition. Its widespread appeal today for some Hindu nationalists and traditionalists comes from this British universalizing of it as common to 'Hinduism' as well as a reaction to Western rule/domination. Practices seen as indigenous were revived, often specifically as they countered norms of the colonial power. An atheist criticism of such practices therefore needs to be aware that it was actually the secular, colonial and political context which created it, where a dominated people sought ways to assert their identity against an oppressive regime. If it is objected that it is religion which allows the practice and legitimates it, it needs to also be considered that the religion was itself created through the secular practice and imposition of law codes and classification norms on India, which made it religious. In the context of medieval Rajasthan, where it was, perhaps, most prevalent, we see a primarily social class and militaristic-based practice of warrior rulers (very occasionally) demanding that wives die alongside their warrior husbands, being transformed into something else. Certainly, this is not to deny that there is a religious problem now, but it relates to something often not inherent in the religion as a whole; rather, we need to face wider structural issues about the way that cultural identities are often embedded in patriarchally dominated societies through women's bodies. Male control is thereby maintained by making something a question of culture, religion or nature which must be preserved. Simply criticizing religion neither gets to the root of the problem nor does it deal with the maintenance and continuation of patterns of male domination, which are as prevalent outside religious institutions as inside them.

Box 6.3

Feminism and gender constructionism

The Enlightenment emphasis on the common rationality of all *men* was extended by some, but not all, to include *women*. Stressing intellectual equality made all other differences unimportant. While concerned with the rights of women across society, religious traditions were critiqued for portraying women in an inferior light. However, Enlightenment feminism (aka First Wave feminism) was itself attacked by those who argued that it subjected women to essentially a masculinist system, wherein rationality and intellect were stressed over embodiment and emotion as ideals. To understand this we must engage the system that gave these norms of male and female in the West (but some similar patterns can be found elsewhere). From the Greeks onwards, especially in the thought of Plato, the male had been constructed as the ideal: rationality and other positively eulogized qualities were seen as masculine; the body, emotion and other negatively perceived qualities were characterized as feminine. The latter, Plato argued, entrapped and corrupted the rational mind. This Greek ideal was absorbed by Christianity and much of the Enlightenment. (Notably, Judaism generally lacks this negative attitude to the body – original sin and the corrupt body represent a Greek world view coupled with Roman legalism – Judaism has always seen the joy of sex as a natural part of creation).

Gender constructionism, therefore, examined the way society was influenced by this heritage. Women, it was suggested, like men, were not born but rather made. Society told one group that it was associated with warmth, emotion and compassion and gave them dolls to play with, while the other group was told to be rational, strong and not cry, and they were given toy soldiers. Most radically of all, scholars like Judith Butler denied the very notion of gender as a natural order. Meanwhile, Second Wave feminists stressed the differences of men and women, and blamed the ills of society on patriarchy and the way that men ruled, and they argued that a matriarchal social order would be preferable. Today, many gender theorists think that Butler went too far in emphasizing the construction of gender. It overlooks biological facts. Contemporary naturalist feminism (Third Wave) argues that there are differences, but not essential ones. We have problems when we speak about women having 'masculine' characteristics (being rational), and men needing to get in touch with their 'feminine' side (e.g. they can cry in public). Why do we see one set of categories as inherent or natural to one group? Men can be as compassionate and emotional as women, while women can be as brave and rational as men. Reason is not masculine, nor compassion feminine. We should also reject the gender antagonism of some earlier feminism.

Patriarchy, gender and society

Religion fits interestingly into debates on gender (see Box 6.3). On the one hand, some religious groups, often termed traditionalists, oppose feminism. For instance, some Christians argue that the Genesis narrative of Adam's creation before Eve shows one is placed above the other. Again, the problematic passages attributed to Paul are also cited. Certainly, Christian churches face a problem here, because while trained theologians know that many of the passages are pseudonymous, they are established by tradition as part of scripture and therefore hard to remove. Nevertheless, many churches have taken the step of admitting women into the priesthood. Here, interestingly, in examples like the Anglican Church in the UK, it has been the more theologically literate bishops and priests who more willingly voted for ordaining women to be priests (and later bishops), while the lay members, who often lack that training, were those who most opposed it.

Church tradition has also played with gender in different ways. Medieval images of Jesus, for instance, often portrayed him with milk emitting from his side where the spear pierced him, in scenes of the crucifixion, which evidently use imagery of Jesus as the mother who nourishes with his/her milk. Indeed, some readings of Genesis in Hebrew also suggest that the original 'man' *adama* was actually a hermaphrodite: the female was not created after; rather, the original was divided. What is termed Queer Theology has expounded many other examples of the way that the natural borders of gender are not stable in religious traditions. This, it is argued, gives evidence that the normal boundaries of society have traditionally found a place that can be challenged within religious traditions (discussed further below).

Again, despite most religious traditions prioritizing male lineages and leadership, they also provided important support and escape mechanisms for women. For instance, in most pre-modern societies the only place where women who were trapped in unhappy marriages, or wished not to marry, could seek refuge was within the monastic life or other forms of communal living for women. While traditional hagiography (the lives of saints) paints many portraits of women so consumed by devotion to Jesus (or in other contexts, the Buddha, and so forth), that they could not bear the idea of marriage and therefore wished to become nuns, instead it is quite possible that a number of these stories are concerned with the options open to those who for whatever reasons wished not to marry, nor to marry their chosen partners. Quite problematically, but showing that gender was not stable within religion, many of these women ascetics were praised for becoming 'male' in their turn to the monastic ideal and having overcome the weakness of their gender. This is part of the Greek legacy that Christianity inherited, and which passed to later Enlightenment, secular and atheist traditions (see Box 6.3). Western society as a whole has often valorized a particular male image and downplayed the body, which is not unique nor particularly attributable to religion/Christianity, but comes strongly from Plato's rationalist Greek philosophical heritage, as well as other sources. A one-sided portrayal of religion as only oppressing women neglects that, for many centuries, it also provided often the only opportunity women could get. Certainly not just in Europe, but also in Asia and elsewhere, across a variety of religious traditions, monasticism in various forms, or women's communities of devotion, provided an outlet for women. Indeed, in institutions like Beguinages (see Box 6.4), women found in religion the only resource available from things like forced marriage, patriarchal oppression (from what we may broadly term secular and not just religious institutions and expectations) and freedom.

Box 6.4

Beguines, female monasticism and withdrawal
Across medieval Europe, a movement called the Beguines was very strong, which saw communities of women banding together to live in houses and sheltered areas in contexts where no men were allowed. Some of these Beguinages, as they were called, grew and became prosperous. In some old cities across Europe the settlements still exist, which were in effect towns within towns containing their own dwellings, churches and industries, and were often self-contained. Eventually, they were suppressed by the Church and the civil authorities as a challenge to patriarchal power. In China, a movement focused around a significant Buddhist deity (technically, a *bodhisattva*, but effectively a deity and often referred to as 'the Chinese Goddess of Compassion'), Guanyin, likewise provided women with a route out of unwanted marriages or similar situations. These generally lay (not monastic or priestly) devotional communities allowed women the rights and freedom to be something other than vehicles for the creation of male heirs, which was expected of them in much of the rest of society.

In pre-modern periods, women often held significant positions of authority in religions. As noted, women seemed to have been prominent leaders and teachers in the early Jesus movement, while later a figure like Hilda of Whitby (614–680), an abbess in early medieval England, was one of the most powerful people in the kingdom. Certainly, religion was complicit in the patriarchal suppression of women's movements, and after a while, women's leadership became far less common in the Church. Indeed, groups which had female leaders tended to be oppressed by the Church as heretical groups. Again, the witch trials of the early modern period focused mainly, but not exclusively, on women; we must not forget, however, that a not insignificant number of men were burnt as well. As stated at the outset, institutional religion has, on the whole, a poor record in its treatment of women, but the situation is far from outright oppression. Furthermore, in quite a few instances, we see quite prominent positions for women in the early phases of a number of religions, with much more freedom than the surrounding society, that is, rights, freedoms and roles that eventually would become suppressed as the surrounding patriarchal cultures closed down these avenues. Indeed, this means religious institutions form one of the main bastions of patriarchy and the denial of women's rights in various areas.

There are, though, contemporary instances where we see religious traditions having a more positive approach towards women and female sexuality. As noted, Daoism is one tradition where women have been extolled as potentially more spiritually gifted. Meanwhile, contemporary Pagan traditions often put emphasis on women's roles and focus on goddess traditions as emphasizing women's spirituality. While we are not talking about the mainstream religions here, it may be seen as indicative of the fact that being religious is not in and of itself inherently negative towards women; traditions can be created where women have at least equal access and roles and where female role models and women's spirituality are given a central place.

As mentioned, a male-dominated society is not limited solely to religious institution and traditions. Many surveys have shown that men still tend to dominate in areas from business to science, academia to government. The World Economic Forum estimated in 2015 that the gender pay gap may take 118 years to close: only by 2133 will women receive equal pay! The same month it was revealed that the UK average pay gap was 14.2% and a shocking 55% for the very top earners. It is hard to attribute this to religion. Indeed, one area often claimed as a bastion of atheism and freethinking and the area most divorced from religion, science, sees very heavily entrenched inequality. Many female scientists have complained of the 'lad's culture' of science labs and working practices and expectations which disadvantage them. Amongst leading scientists we do not see women more equally represented than in other comparable fields, and often they are less represented. Indeed, even in the twenty-first century, some male scientists have suggested that women simply may not be up to the job or the equal of males. To see sexism and inequality as solely the realm of religion is to hide from the sad fact that our cultures and societies are rife with endemic sexism, and that atheists and religious believers both engage in practices and mindsets that are not attuned to solving the problem.

THINKING ABOUT GENDER AND BODIES TODAY

Does this mean that religion today is inherently opposed to gender equality because despite moments when it has been supportive, this has always been within the context of wider suppression? Certainly Mary Daly (mentioned above) thought so and therefore broke away from the Church. Other women who wish for some form of spirituality have turned to goddesses and have sought to create, or recreate, a matriarchal goddess spirituality that draws inspiration from historical perspectives. For many of these goddess worshippers, the goddess does not necessarily represent a 'reality' out there, but rather acts as a form of archetype or inspirational model from which they can draw inspiration. Here we see what may be spoken of as consciously atheist forms of religion. Meanwhile, as mentioned, some within traditional religions have sought to go back to foundations which are actually quite pro-feminist. Many progressive religious groups have agendas which are fully in accord with secular movements in feminism and other areas.

It may also be suggested that contemporary thinking around gender may benefit from some of the examples found within religious traditions. As mentioned, religions hold resources for seeing gender as going beyond the fixed categories (of Western thought). As such, it could hold resources in different ways in terms of art, countercultural examples and theory for gender theorists and those who wish to reject male/female as two fixed and identifiably different identity options. One example of this would be the words of a proponent and founder in the field of Queer Theology, Professor Elizabeth Stuart:

> Growing up surrounded by men wearing clothes society labelled feminine whom I had to relate to as "father," taught by women who were my "sisters" or "mothers" with names such as Augustine and Bernard Joseph taught me that societal categories were not fixed, that they could be played around with and that the Church was a place in which gender shifted.

Nevertheless, I suspect that around areas of gender, sexuality and embodiment, it is likely that continuing battles will be waged between secular societies and religious institutions; individual atheists and individual religious adherents; and also, internally within religious and secular/atheist traditions. Some of this will be about the question of whether any particular tradition represents the true nature, or essence, of these religions, while rival interpretations are disputed and discussed as to what to make of the available evidence. However, what is important to realize is that the evidence is mixed and does not point simply to any religion having any one stance, opinion or attitude around questions of gender, sexuality and embodiment.

As we have mentioned, traditions like Judaism have not tended to see sex as something taboo or shameful, which is one way that the Christian tradition, historically and still today in some places, has portrayed it. In this Judaism is not alone, as Zoroastrianism has also seen reproduction as something positive, an area where humanity can work in concert with the benevolent creator deity in the production of life. Today, goddess traditions and Paganism also tend to see sex as natural and therefore a part of the positive creative urge within the world and to be celebrated. This, of course, is not to deny that many religious traditions have not given people feelings of shame about their sexual nature or expressions of it, but it is far from being the only way that religion can look at this question. Indeed, once again, control of sexuality and especially female fertility is never simply a 'religious' issue but is also bound into the nexus of patriarchal society, group identity and power relations between individuals and groups. The deplorable use of rape as a weapon of war is a sure sign of the way that this is used to control, diminish and stamp authority upon those defeated. Rarely, if ever, does such action have (official/justified) religious blessing.

A final area to mention, or return to, is that sexism is not something confined to religion or religious traditions; rather, it seems endemic in many areas of society, whether in politics, academia, journalism, the media or almost any other area. While some may suggest that this is because of religion, it seems very hard to justify such a viewpoint, because on the one hand, as we have discussed, it is very hard to show whether any influence goes from religion to a wider culture, or from that wider culture to religion. Certainly, this seems to cut both ways. While certain religious texts may justify a continued male privilege in many contexts, it cannot be seen as a controlling factor across the whole of every society and sphere of life. On the other hand, areas like contemporary science, which seem to have a glass ceiling, are not directly affected by religion, nor does such bias find any justification through religious narratives; rather, we are talking about ways of working and attitudes which are embedded more widely in people's mindsets and ways of doing things. This does not, of course, excuse religious traditions in any way for their implication in many centuries of male patriarchal control, but we cannot opt for simple answers to define problems.

7

HUMAN ANIMALS, NON-HUMAN ANIMALS AND THE UNIVERSE AROUND US

○ ○ ○

THE SCHOLARLY BIT

I write this chapter fully confessing that my background is not in the physical sciences, but in the humanities and social sciences. Nevertheless, it is important that we tackle the disputes on and around the cosmos, evolution and the scientific evidence. I shall do this in a particular way, which will be to relate and discuss the debates rather than adjudicating or pontificating on the scientific evidence. There are several main themes we need to cover here: 1) the question of whether science and religion are friends or enemies (which will involve a review of the history of the relationship and development of the two); 2) evolution and creationism (assessing the debate between these two clashing perspectives); and 3) design, creation and the cosmos (which is asking about the evidence and place for any argument for or against the deity today in relation to notions of design and what we know about the universe).

Religion and science: Friends or foes?

It is common to hear from the atheist side today that religion has always opposed science and is stuck in a primitive world view and not adaptable to change. Even, on a more nuanced view, it may be argued that while religion and science may have had some links in the past, today they are inevitably in conflict. To start, let me state my point of view, which is that there is no necessary conflict; however, this does not change the fact that conflicts have arisen, but the reasons both for this and the conflicts themselves are complicated. Importantly, though, we need to realize that we are also engaged in an anachronistic discussion. What we today call 'science' and 'religion' have not historically existed as separable spheres. The modern so-called physical sciences are a development from natural philosophy, which was as much a moral as a 'scientific' realm, while both what we now call 'philosophy' and 'science' were intertwined with that other modern category 'religion' in numerous ways in most historical periods. We must proceed, then, recognizing that our terms will skew the way we look at history. With that said, we explore together the history, looking mainly at Europe since the Middle Ages but bringing in other periods and regions.

We start in ancient Greece as modern reason and science often see their roots there. Today, Aristotle (384–322 BCE) is sometimes portrayed as an enemy of the scientific world view, but such a standpoint ignores the historical evidence. For the sake of simplicity we can contrast two strands in Greek/Western philosophy: Plato's (c. 429–347 BCE) idealism and Aristotle's empiricism. Idealism emphasizes ideas and abstract concepts and principles, arguing that true knowledge is largely detached from the world, which for Plato is a snare to our senses and intellect. Empiricism, exemplified by Aristotle, argues that we know things only through the world, taking the evidence of our eyes and physical experience seriously. Empiricism, as well as being a philosophical school, provides the foundation for science in the Western world (supplemented by discoveries from elsewhere as we discuss below).

Aristotle's observations of the world and the human body were, for centuries, amongst the most detailed and important for developing physical science. Largely lost to Europe for centuries, Aristotle's philosophy returned in the Middle Ages inspiring an intellectual revolution. Historians of thought have spoken of a twelfth-century Renaissance, and while too simplistic to attribute this simply to the rediscovery of Aristotle, a new interest in the physical world and science was beginning to flourish in the period we call the Renaissance (c. fourteenth to sixteenth century CE), and then from there until today. Aristotle's method was a key part, therefore, in the moves towards the foundation of modern science. Given the period, it should be no surprise that the majority of these early scientists in Europe were Christians, though others were Jewish (we discuss Islam below). They believed that the world had been created by a designer who instilled purpose and order into the universe; therefore, it could be understood. This idea was key to the exploration of science. Amongst the renowned scientists was someone whose ideas are still invoked today, William of Ockham (1285–1347), in particular his famous concept of Ockham's razor (see Box 7.1).

Box 7.1

Ockham's razor and God's existence

Still used as a principle of science today, Ockham's razor is that wherever possible we should prefer the simpler answer, or that which requires fewer complications, than the opposite. Indeed, today atheist scientists will use it as an argument against God: the simple answer is that the universe is just a natural phenomenon; the complicated answer is that it requires an additional element, a creator.

Ockham's razor suggests we have a universe with no creator, and therefore no God. Importantly, however, Ockham himself was, while a scientist, first and foremost a Christian theologian. He was, in fact, a Franciscan friar, and his famous razor was developed by him as a theological principle. Indeed, in Ockham's hands the razor was originally designed as an argument for God's existence! The argument, in brief, went something like this: to explain that there is something, the simple answer is that an all-powerful being created it; the complex answer is that we create theories and hypotheses which inevitably multiply and seek to explain the complexity of the world by being more complex than the phenomenon. I am not going to suggest which one is more compelling as an argument just yet; rather, for those who argue that theology and religion are irrational and always against science and reason, the onus is to explain how and why the latter pair employ a theological principle as a central concept. Ockham's razor, as mentioned, remains central in science. It is also a key idea in philosophy.

It has been argued that the rise of modern science is due to theologians (who were also scientists) who believed that the world was rational and so could be investigated scientifically, and certainly, on a historical basis it is hard to avoid this. The base upon which modern science stands would never have developed if they hadn't existed. Now, it might be argued that science has moved on and so while this heritage exists, it is irrelevant to whether religion and science are in harmony or conflict today. But as my example of Ockham's razor shows, such a standpoint would be too simple: science today still employs a theological principle as a key concept, or at least something originally developed as a theological principle (even if both philosophers and the scientific community tend to claim it as 'their' idea). Perhaps more mutuality exists than might be supposed?

This history, however, would not be complete if we only discuss Europe. In China many key developments had taken place with gunpowder, the magnet and paper all having been developed there. Indeed, the historian of science, Joseph Needham, has convincingly argued that many of these developments were due to Daoism in particular, and the interests of that tradition in exploring the world. Therefore, ideas about Europe's central role can be disputed, as China's so-called Three Great Inventions were central:

- Paper allowed ideas to be printed and spread: while China developed printing centuries before it was 'discovered' in Europe, the latter mechanized the process further allowing unrivalled dissemination (comparable to today's Internet revolution).

- The magnet allowed navigation and the 'age of discovery', which gave Europe the money, raw materials and further knowledge and resources to take advantage of the beginnings of what became the scientific revolution. (Of course, no place was actually 'discovered', people were already there, while the next invention was key to Europe's power claims in this regard.)

- Gunpowder was developed most fully in Europe to create weaponry and allowed the domination of the globe – though China, contrary to what some think, did not simply make fireworks but developed rockets and other weaponry, but due to the geographical and political context, it was not exploited for conquest nor advanced through the 'arms race' that Europe's divided and warring small kingdoms encouraged.

China, though, is only another part of the story, and also of central importance is the Muslim-majority world.

Greek science and philosophy, while largely lost to Western Europe, were preserved first in the Greek-speaking Christian world but then were developed and advanced by the Muslim cultures of the Middle East as the great Islamic empires of the age expanded. Older, and biased, histories of science tend to paint the Islamic contribution as essentially passing on the Greek heritage with a few technical additions, but it is clear from contemporary historical studies that it was far more. (For a discussion of why modern science did not therefore develop, see Box 7.2.) The fact that many of our English words for scientific fields have Arabic origins is no accident: chemistry comes from *al-kemia* and algebra from *al-jabr*, areas which were very much pioneered in the Middle East. Meanwhile, optics were also developed and improved there. The telescopes that saw the European advances in astronomy were made using lenses at first imported from the Islamic world and then refined using the technology learnt from there. That the Renaissance first occurred in Italy is no accident: Venetian and Florentine trade routes across the Mediterranean facilitated the exchange of technology and knowledge from Muslim merchants and scholars.

Box 7.2

Why didn't the Islamic world develop modern science?
Why was it Europe that developed modern science if it was the Islamic world that was originally so far ahead? The scientist Neil deGrasse Tyson argues that it was due to one man: Abu Hamid Muhammad ibn Muhammed al-Ghazali (c. 1058–1111). al-Ghazali was influential in replacing a form of Islamic theology infused with Greek philosophy and rationalism with more conservative theological thought emphasizing submission to the divine will and the limits of human knowledge, typified in the phrase *bila kayf*, 'without asking why'. Tyson's argument, however, seems limited by several factors:

First, it is not clear that one person could suddenly stop scientific advance dead in its tracks across many regions and, by then, disparate empires. This was the twelfth century, and without the Internet, television and radio ideas travelled slowly, and al-Ghazali's ideas were not at first universally supported. It also seems to hark back to a nineteenth-century view of history of 'great men': heroes (or villains) of thought who shaped the world. It entirely ignores the political and social factors. Second, for centuries, Baghdad had been the unrivalled intellectual capital of the Muslim world. The Bait al-Hikmah (literally 'House of Wisdom'), the world's greatest centre of learning, flourished from the ninth until twelfth centuries, with Islamic, Jewish and Christian scholars working side by side. (This has huge lessons in terms of what multicultural societies produce, a common feature of many eras of major social and intellectual advancement.) Here, great scientific advances came with scholars and ideas converging from as far afield as Europe and China. It was through Baghdad that the Indian discovery of the number '0' was first found to be a major advance and used to develop mathematics more broadly. However, in 1258 Baghdad was sacked by the invading Mongol armies. The slaughter and destruction was immense: historical records speak of the waters of the river Tiber running black with the blood of scholars and the ink of books and scrolls. Many mourn the destruction of the great library of Alexandria and this is comparable. Did this stop the modern scientific revolution from occurring in the Middle East? The greatest scholars, scientists and mathematicians were dead, and the threat of invasion and war meant resources that could have rebuilt were plundered or directed elsewhere. However, the Islamic world did not descend into a dark age, and science remained in later dynasties like the Moghul and Ottoman Empires. Indeed, for several centuries, the Ottoman Empire at least matched, if not surpassed, Europe in some areas in science and engineering. Nevertheless, the centre for scientific discovery moved elsewhere. War, political will and global social trends saw Europe take the lead.

In Renaissance Europe, like the Middle Ages, science and religion were interlinked. Greek-inspired beliefs of mystical ordering in patterns in the universe saw religion remaining an inspiration for science's continued growth. However, science was treated as secret knowledge: only a small literate elite were initiated into its secrets, and individual discoveries were not shared widely. A new model was needed and this emerged with what is sometimes called the Baconian model: science should be shared, not kept in the dark. Therefore, discoveries became available to a wider scientific circle. The founding of the Royal Society in 1660 in London is an aspect of this. This is not to say that science stopped being a religious practice. Francis Bacon (1561–1626) himself, from whom we get the term, wrote about Rosicrucian ideas, a rather secretive set of religious beliefs. Such beliefs were common with founding figures of the Royal Society like Elias Ashmole (1617–1692), also being known to write Rosicrucian prayers, while he and others were also known to be involved in the spiritual side of Masonic practice. Later, scientists like Isaac Newton (1642–1727) were also drawing upon similar religious principles and impulses to seek order in the universe. However, the sharing of knowledge and the open writing of ideas meant that anyone with enough understanding and literacy could become part of the community of science.

As literacy progressed throughout the eighteenth, nineteenth and twentieth centuries, the scientific world was simply drawing upon a wider body of practitioners. The scientific discoveries of these centuries and the exponential growth in knowledge are not related to a freedom of science from the grips of religious dogmatism; rather, it seems, it is about an increase in literacy and the concept, first expounded by very religious thinkers, that science should be shared and open to all, not the secret knowledge of a small elite. Tied to this are developments in printing, which allowed ideas to be spread reliably and at speed. Notably, these new advances saw Bacon's own method, of science as induction, replaced by science as deduction, which was also crucial: but the Baconian model (not method) meant this was widely shared, facilitating science's growth and development.

While we may establish that religious people have been involved in science, and that religious beliefs and impulses have helped develop it, and even that scientists today still use at least one theological concept to underpin the modern discipline (see Box 7.1), various debates may show that religion actually holds science back and must eventually be in conflict.

We will now explore two case studies, first concerning evolution and creationism, and then concerning design arguments and the cosmos, arguments that both figure a famous central character: Charles Darwin (1809–1882) and Galileo Galilei (1564–1642), respectively.

Darwin, evolution and creationism

The story of Darwin's expeditions on the Beagle and his writing of *On The Origin of Species* are well known, so we need not spend time repeating this. However, a lot of mythology surrounds the man and his story. Several important aspects of this need to be picked up. First, it was not Darwin's discoveries concerning evolution that led him to atheism, but rather, as biographical studies have shown, it was the death of his eldest daughter, Annie Elizabeth. He could not reconcile his belief in an all-loving and all-powerful God with this tragedy (see Chapter 4).

Second, evolution was not even a major reason for most people to lose their faith in God. As far as can be ascertained from the record of nineteenth-century converts to atheism, there were three main factors: increasing literacy, moral revolt and historical studies. While separate, each is linked as we'll see: as people read the Christian Old Testament, they came face to face with a petty, vengeful and often despotic deity. Moral problems with this as well as some doctrines like an eternal hell repelled many people from organized religion, if not all religion. Meanwhile, archaeology and biblical studies showed the Bible was not the reliable source it was once believed to be. Historical studies and simply reading the Bible seem to have led far more people to atheism than any scientific doubts. Indeed, scientific colleagues like Charles Lyell (1797–1875), credited as one of the founders of modern geology, who helped show that the earth was far more than the 6000 or 7000 years a traditional interpretation of the Bible suggested (but not the only or best way of reading it, as we'll see below), did not find evolution (nor geology) a reason to stop being a staunch Christian.

Third, the famous and iconic 1860 debate where Thomas Huxley (1829–1895) faced Samuel Wilberforce (1805–1873) the Bishop of Oxford is not the clear triumph of science over faith many atheist proponents claim. For one thing, Wilberforce was not just the Bishop of Oxford, he was also a vice president of the British Association for the Advancement of Science, which held the debate, and a noted ornithologist in his own right, not simply some ignorant churchman. Huxley meanwhile was not a scientist at all, but simply a spokesperson for the Darwinian viewpoint. For another, the contemporary records we have of the debate tell us that Wilberforce was a powerful orator, while Huxley spoke quietly and was barely audible; even his supporters lamented his performance. As such, it seems possible that Wilberforce actually won the day and even gave a reasoned argument for his position; he had written a review of the *Origin of the Species*, which Darwin himself called 'uncommonly clever' and which 'makes a very telling case against me' and which he subsequently sought to counter by defending the weaknesses in his argument it had observed. The myth that Huxley had won the day and shifted public opinion was spread in Huxley's own account written many years later. We are probably all familiar with a variety of contemporary newspaper cartoons depicting Darwin's head on a monkey's body, which has been seen to reflect something Wilberforce is seen as having said – 'Was it through his grandfather or grandmother that he [Huxley] claimed descent from a monkey?' – but in all likelihood was not said at the debate (if at all). Appearing in the aftermath of the debate, and after Darwin's the *Descent of Man* (1871), such cartoons often mocked Darwin and evolution; that was the public sentiment. It was a number of years before the majority of the scientific community, let alone the public, accepted the theory of evolution.

With some of the mythology cleared away, let's pose two questions. First, was religious belief a hindrance to the acceptance of evolution? I would answer, yes. Scientific orthodoxy of the day relied upon sources like the Bible, which read in a certain way hindered the acceptance of evolution. Indeed, because it was both scientific and religious orthodoxy, it was harder to jettison. Second, does this mean that religion (specifically the Christian Bible and tradition) is opposed to evolution or science? To this I would answer, in principle, no. In Darwin's day, Christian scientists like Lyell were able to accept evolution. Indeed, for decades following, the majority of scientists in places like Europe and North America continued to be Christians, and religious belief predominated amongst scientists in many parts of the world (see Chapter 1). Certainly today it really has to be said that there is no other show in town, and while creationists argue that evolution is 'just a theory', this ignores the overwhelming evidence and support behind it and misinterprets what a scientific 'theory' means. If religion and evolution are not compatible, then it is pretty much a done deal for atheism. Nevertheless, creationism is on the rise, with many Christians (and Muslims) feeling that being a true believer means denying evolution; therefore, it is necessary to show why creationism is badly misguided from a religious point of view, and I'll leave the scientific proof to others who have done it much better than I could.

As discussed in Chapter 2, nobody reads the entirety of any religious book literally. Some parts are clearly symbolic. Indeed, a very significant strand in Christian theology has held that the Bible should primarily be read for symbolic and ethical messages. The emphasis on reading it *only* in a literal way is very modern. Those who wrote these scriptural texts would be bemused to say the least. Even literalists don't read it all literally: nobody, for instance, reads 'Jesus is the lamb of God' as a statement about Jesus' ovine nature. Likewise, many parts have often been seen as purely symbolic; the love imagery of the Song of Songs was traditionally read as an allegory of God's love for the soul, for instance, but today Christians generally see it (probably as it was written) as discussing romantic love. Which bits people think are symbolic and which bits are literal is contextual. It cannot be asserted that the only, or most traditional, Christian reading of Genesis is a literal one. However, more than this, the specific literal reading that denies evolution comes from an English translation. The Hebrew term translated as 'days', as in 'God created the world in six days' (don't forget he rested on the seventh), while it can literally mean one 24-hour period (day and night), is actually far looser and means a period of time which could be thousands of years, or even unspecified durations. The denial of evolution and its time frame of millions of years, which is seen as being in contradiction to the Bible, is actually therefore only in contradiction to a poor *translation* of the Bible.

The Bible needs to be interpreted in context, which is not simply a modern liberal tradition. We discussed slavery previously, noting that despite the Bible clearly allowing slavery, evangelical Christians (those we may most expect to read the Bible literally) argued that while slavery was part of its content, it was not the true message. Passages permitting slavery were seen as overruled by the greater message of equality. This led to the fight against slavery that saw it first banned within the British context. We should expect the biblical authors to reflect the world view of their times, including scientific claims. As such, even if Genesis denied the time periods needed for evolution, this would not mean that Christians today are bound by such claims. As with slavery, an overall meaning can override specific literal/contextual claims. Indeed, many Christians read the Genesis creation narrative more metaphorically, suggesting that God laid the system on which evolution works. This fully aligns with the tradition of interpretation and contextualization found in Christianity for centuries. Others even argue that reading it this way stretches the idea that it contains scientific truths too far, suggesting it should be read for other truths, such as ethical ones. As we will see when we discuss Galileo below, such an argument is not a modern liberal enlightenment response but one which is centuries old. Indeed, one of Christianity's first theologians, Origen (c. 184–254 CE) (see Chapter 2), said Genesis should not be read literally, targeting what he termed 'ignorant' Christians who said God really walked in the Garden of Eden. This shows again that arguing that only a literal reading is 'traditional' is simply nonsense.

Creationism can actually be argued to be the recent innovation, a concept reactive to modernity that reads the Bible as literal facts and scientific claims (see Chapter 2). A different reading of the Bible exists in traditional resources to read it metaphorically and symbolically, while also realizing that it is written from a particular context. This does not claim that none of the text is literal, nor that symbolic readings always take precedence, as major theologians from Jerome (347–420) to Thomas Aquinas (1225–1274) have stressed the literal over the symbolic. However, which bits are read in which ways has varied throughout history. Similar claims could be made by Muslims for the Qur'an. Of course, for most of the past 2000 years, Christians have, even if taking it symbolically, assumed at the same time that the Genesis account contains literal facts; however, this reflects the available world view. Nevertheless, some atheist critics polemically suggested that if the Bible, or other religious books, actually contained things which have only been made known through modern science, then they would believe it was revelation. However, this suggests a very simplistic understanding of the books – although one that responds to the often loudly proclaimed, but equally simplistic, notions of evangelical or fundamentalist believers. As discussed in Chapter 2, these texts are human constructions which reflect the time and context of their writers. Given this, even if the deity had revealed advanced scientific knowledge by a divine voice, the human scribes presumably would have not recorded it as relevant, or understandable, at that time! In fact, Christian theology even argues for this contextualism. Almost 500 years ago, John Calvin (1509–1564) suggested that when God revealed the scriptures it was in ways and terms applicable to the people and their context, a theory termed 'accomodationism'. This was long before anyone imagined a conflict between science and religion. Of course, models of scripture as being the direct and infallible words of a divine being persist in many religious traditions, but it is never the only reading, nor always the most orthodox one, and certainly not the one that fits the historical record.

Galileo, design and Aristotle

As we come to Galileo, we will actually see a further claim made by Christians in his time, so long before the modern era and the Enlightenment. This claim is that the Bible and Christianity gave moral and spiritual truths, while scientific truths may be found elsewhere. Although widely accepted by many progressive Christians today, it can be controversial from two standpoints. On the one hand, evangelical and fundamentalist Christians often see it as a modern or Enlightenment view of liberal Christians. On the other hand, atheist critics like Jerry Coyne have claimed it is only modern 'liberal' forms of religion which make such claims. However, as we have seen, it goes back hundreds of years and has antecedents in the way (see Chapter 2) that religions have always selectively read their scriptures and understood them in relation to the prevailing world view. It assumes that religions must and should be unchanging systems fixed in one age, which is not what the history of religions shows. Another important aspect of this debate is that the mythology of the event often portrays Galileo's observations that the earth revolved around the sun as a dispute of science against religion. But, as with many things, it is far more complicated than that. We can see Galileo's discoveries and those of his contemporaries, supported by some Christians but not others.

The backdrop to Galileo's work was Reformation Europe. The Protestant tradition had arisen and spilt a once-united European Christendom. In response, the Roman Catholic Church sought to regroup and regain the high ground in the debate. Fundamental in this was the so-called Council of Trent (1545–1563) (actually a series of events over many years) where the Catholic Church rethought its position on many issues. One key point it established was founding its theology on what is called Thomism, the thought of Thomas Aquinas. He used the person who at that time was becoming the most highly regarded philosopher, Aristotle. The Roman Catholic Church therefore tied its intellectual credibility to a defence of Aristotle's philosophy as interpreted by Aquinas (or, to be more accurate, the Muslim interpretation of Aristotle by Ibn Sina (980–1037), which Aquinas took on). However, Aristotle's role in formulating the basis of scientific method, as we discussed, would also be his undoing as Galileo's observations were understood to challenge Aristotle. However, it was another figure whose ideas about the cosmos were more directly challenged: Claudius Ptolemaeus, known as Ptolemy (c. 90–168 CE). Ptolemy's *Almagest* offered the most cogent arguments for an earth-centred universe. That his views were dominant for almost 1500 years should give us some pause for thought. By explaining the rotation of the planets by 'eccentric' circles, his system actually made sense of what could be observed without advanced telescopes. Only with more powerful telescopes, coming from Islamic optical advances, could Galileo show that the Ptolemaic system didn't work.

Galileo was not, though, the first person to suggest a heliocentric universe. The argument had been made by another Greek scientist, Aristarchus (c. 310–230 BCE); however, he could offer no rationale for how this happened. Therefore, Ptolemy's system, which made more sense of the available evidence, was preferred. We should also remember that Galileo himself could not actually explain the alternative system, the Copernican model with the sun at the centre. This system was named after Nicholas Copernicus (1473–1543) who was the first in the modern world to defend heliocentrism (a sun-centred cosmos). Copernicus was himself a priest, being a canon at Frombork Cathedral, and did a lot of his work at Varmia, where his uncle was a bishop. Indeed, when he published his main ideas in 1542, he dedicated it to Pope Paul III. This was not done in opposition to the Church; rather, it was seen as calendrically useful, and a German priest he was in conversation with, Andreas Osiander (1498–1552), hailed it as mathematically useful (even if untrue physically).

In due course, Copernicus' heliocentrism came to be opposed by the Church on the grounds that it opposed the Bible, but also because it opposed Ptolemy, whose system, as mentioned, had worked to make sense of the world based upon known observations for around 1500 years. This was not just anti-intellectualism; indeed, Copernicus was also opposed by the universities who argued that he opposed Aristotle and Ptolemy, while the leading astronomers of his day argued that he opposed Ptolemy. However, Copernicus was largely ignored, and while some atheist proponents note that one supporter of heliocentrism, Giordano Bruno (1548–1600), was burnt as a heretic, this is almost certainly because he held very unorthodox theological views. The files on his trial are now missing, so we can't know exactly what condemned him to death; nevertheless, contemporary accounts show far more interest in his theology than his rather fringe astronomical views. Indeed, in terms of scientific history, we need to remember that the Copernican revolution, as we call it, was not a revolution in his own day. There were simply two competing views: the Ptolemaic earth-centred system and the Copernican heliocentric system. Galileo's signal contribution with improved telescopic technology was to show that the Ptolemaic system was wrong: he could offer a disproof that Copernicus could not. However, Copernicus' system didn't offer an entirely viable alternative, for neither Copernicus nor Galileo could show how a heliocentric view actually worked. Indeed, in 1574, a Danish astronomer called Tycho Brahe (1546–1601) would show that both Ptolemy and Copernicus had got their calculations wrong; however, not being a mathematician, he couldn't work out the correct orbits. Opposition to heliocentrism was not, then, at first purely dogmatism and refusal to accept a new argument. It took a while for the system to be shown to be viable, although this did happen during Galileo's lifetime. However, it was not Galileo himself who did this, and we had to wait until Johannes Kepler (1571–1630) published his *Epitome Astromoniae Copernicae* (1618–1621) for a heliocentric system with altered orbits which actually showed how it could work. (He notably named his book after Copernicus, recognizing his role in the development of the heliocentric model.) Indeed, Kepler saw his discoveries as a sign of God's design in the universe because of what he saw as the mathematical beauty of the system he had discovered.

The scientific debate is therefore far more contested and complex than the ordinary story.

Although Galileo was accused of violating biblical teachings on the cosmos, it is not entirely clear if this was the main reason why the Catholic Church condemned him. Both Brahe and Kepler were free to conduct their work; indeed, their Protestant rulers even funded and supported their work – in Protestant Europe, that the earth moved round the sun was readily accepted. That is why this argument is best seen as not being about a challenge to the Bible, but a challenge to an established order, which included Aristotle. The Protestants were quite relaxed that while what they saw as the symbolic language of the Bible written many centuries before, might not accurately reflect the latest knowledge about science and the cosmos – for some, this would be explained by Calvin's theory of accommodationism noted above – they welcomed evidence that Aristotle, and therefore the foundation of the Catholic Church, might be at fault. The suppression of Galileo's teachings by the Roman Catholic Church is more plausibly understood, not because it necessarily went against the Bible (if so, the Protestants also would have opposed it) but because it challenged a particular tradition which they supported. Central in this, ideologically, was the work of Aristotle. Unfairly, therefore, Aristotle has become a symbol of those standing against science, but he is just a pawn invoked in power games between opposing world views. If some of the key events in Galileo's disputes with the ecclesiastical authorities are examined, it will be seen that we do not simply see a religion-versus-science debate (see Box 7.3).

Box 7.3

Galileo's trials
In 1611 Galileo was for the first time questioned on his views, though this was not about cosmology. He had argued for Archimedes over Aristotle in an issue on which they disagreed in front of the Roman Catholic cardinals, and was defended there by Cardinal Maffeo Barberini, who would later become Pope Urban VIII, as well as his patron. He was therefore known for challenging Aristotle, which, as we have mentioned, was problematic for the Church, as it had based its intellectual credibility on defending Thomas Aquinas' Aristotelian-based theology, Thomism. As such,

it is no surprise that when a public complaint was levelled against him in 1615 by a friar called Niccolo Lorini, Galileo was first brought to trial where a consultation to the Office of the Inquisition declared heliocentrism heretical. It was at this stage, in fact, that Copernicus' *De Revolutionibus* was put on the Index of Prohibited Books. When it remained simply an interesting mathematical puzzle, it had not seemingly bothered the Church; as noted, Copernicus could offer no proofs nor even disprove Ptolemy. Now, however, Copernicus' ideas were politically dangerous. Notably, though, at this stage one of Galileo's supporters, Cardinal Bellarmine, was clear that Galileo himself was not put on trial nor condemned, although he warned him not to write about Copernicus. In 1630, however, Galileo wrote his famous *Dialogue Concerning the Two Chief World Systems*, meaning Ptolemaic and Copernican. In that work, two characters – Salviati, who is portrayed as open-minded, and Simplicio, a Ptolemaist but suspected of representing of one-time friend and patron Urban VIII – debate. While Salviati wins at the end of the book, he gives way to Simplicio. It was printed in 1631, but Urban suspended printing the following year and Galileo was brought before the Inquisition with Urban himself presiding. In 1633 Galileo admitted making the Copernican case too strong and promised to amend the book. While the Church forced Galileo to back down on pain of death (because heliocentrism was declared a heresy), he could not actually prove his position. It was also not the end of his studies. Condemned for lesser charges than heresy, he was placed very pleasantly under house arrest by one of the Catholic cardinals, who ensured he had what he needed to continue his scientific studies.

Notably, neither Cardinal Bellarmine, a Catholic leader and supporter of Galileo, nor Galileo saw these scientific studies as an attack upon Christianity. Neither man was an atheist; rather, they saw science as providing knowledge about the world, and religion as providing ethical and spiritual guidance. We therefore do not see a straightforward battle of science against religion; rather, the same scientific discoveries were lauded by some and decried by others because of different ideological and power games at work. It is also notable that while Pope John Paul II publically apologized for the condemnation against Galileo in 1992, the *Dialogue* had been published by the Catholic Church in 1744, and in 1758 it allowed Copernicus' books to be read, with the *Dialogue* taken off the Index of Prohibited Books in 1835. As such, these scientific views are entirely compatible with Roman Catholicism, while the only opponents are contemporary flat-earthers, who tend to be creationists too. They are normally in the Protestant camp; however, the flat-earth proponents are a very fringe and marginal group. What this shows, though, is that opposition to science, or certain scientific principles, are not inherent in any religious group. Just as Catholics were resisting heliocentrism in Galileo's time, it was being allowed to be freely taught, even having research funded, by Protestants. Meanwhile, in the contemporary context, while Pope John Paul II apologized for ever condemning Galileo, and admitted the Church's mistake, and Pope Francis has led the Catholic Church in supporting climate change, it is often (American) evangelical Protestants who are climate-change deniers and sceptics (although this may be far from representative of Protestantism, or even evangelicalism, as a whole globally). Again, opposition to climate change may often be as much linked to certain political and economic agendas in businesses like oil and the automotive industry, as it is to religion. Simplistic black-and-white, religion-versus-science explanations generally do not tend to help us understand what is going on in these debates.

THINKING ABOUT 'CREATURES' AND 'CREATION' TODAY

Historically, to suggest any inherent or traditional battle between science and religion is misguided (see Box 7.4); rather, contemporary science owes its origins, foundations and even much of its contemporary basis to developments made by religious people often operating in explicitly theological terms. This is not to say, though, that all religion is amenable to science, as contemporary flat-earthers are downright antagonistic and opposed. But this is not the only stance and is certainly not inherent. Arguably, though, contemporary science becomes anti-religion inherently because it removes the necessity for any religious world view.

Box 7.4

Has there always been a war between science and religion?

The concept that religion and science have been constantly at loggerheads was first proposed in two nineteenth-century texts – John William Draper's *History of the Conflict Between Religion and Science* (1875) and Andrew Dickson's *A History of the Warfare of Science with Theology in Christendom* (1896) – which popularized this idea. While historians of science have long shown the errors and misrepresentation in the concept, it remains commonplace, and even some well-educated atheists present this as fact. For instance, Jerry Coyne's *Faith vs. Fact: Why Science and Religion Are Incompatible* (2015) introduces these texts in the first pages to set up his argument. However, the origins of science arose in places like China as very much part of what may be termed alchemical experiments in Chinese religious thought. Ancient Greece is another place and Coyne claims this as a secular origin. However, he cites figures like Aristotle and Pythagoras, who were far from atheists. Aristotle originated what Aquinas took up as the so-called first-cause argument for God's existence: there must have been some uncaused cause behind the universe. Aristotle was a deist. Pythagoras, meanwhile, was not primarily known in ancient Greece as a mathematician, but rather as the founder of a religious group that believed in reincarnation and employed mathematics to explain the mystical ordering of the cosmos and its relation to an inner spiritual life. Indeed, until at least the Renaissance, and certainly for Newton, mathematical patterns in the universe were a sign of its divine design and order. This is not to deny that some like Pliny the Elder (23–79 CE) were deeply sceptical of religion; however, tracing science back to a 'secular' Greek source does not hold. Regardless of the origins, it is clear that science flourished in both the medieval Christian and Islamic worlds, and as discussed above, this is what laid the foundations of what becomes modern science, which drew from China, Greece, India and the Middle East before the scientific revolution of the past few centuries in Europe. However, as discussed above, this revolution was not about freeing science from religious control but seems to have been connected historically to the rise of literacy and the free sharing of knowledge. Of course, at times religious authorities did battle against some scientific innovations, but as we have seen this is not simply about religion as some generic thing always wanting to block science, but instead is tied to more complicated cultural and political battles. Furthermore, as discussed at the start of this chapter, we cannot find separate spheres of 'religion' and 'science' in the historical record. The views of Pythagoras and Newton are examples where mathematics and the physical world are part and parcel of the spiritual and religious quest. To separate them does violence to the self-understanding of each.

Some say that the first person to strongly present this case was Jean-Baptiste Lamarck (1744–1829), who when presenting a copy of his scientific book to the Emperor Napoleon (1769–1821) was queried as to why no mention of God could be found within the text. His reply was simple: 'I have no need of that hypothesis'. Other sources suggest this remark was made by Paul-Henri Thiry Holbach (known as Baron d'Holbach) (1723–1789); however, the whole story is likely to be apocryphal. Certainly, in the Middle Ages, belief in God would be entirely rational: there was no other way to explain why we are here, why life is like it is and why beauty exists in the world. The development of cosmology and physics have shown, however, that we can explain many of the workings of the universe by entirely physical means. Perhaps most important, though, is Darwin. How can we explain something as complicated as the eye or brain? Here, evolution provides the key; indeed, we can see in nature examples of various stages of the development of things like eyes (sensors and filters for light, shade and images) that allow us to see how gradual changes could develop. Given the advances in science so far, after only a very short period in human history since the scientific revolution began, we must expect further advances to explain much more. As such, it is entirely credible to see why an atheist can say of God that they simply have no need of that 'hypothesis'. However, does this mean that religion must be abandoned? Just because it is credible to have one world view, atheism, does not mean that you must be credulous to have another world view (see Chapters 1 and 8).

As discussed, religion and science are not necessarily opposed. For hundreds of years, religious scientists and educated religious people have found very feasible ways that make full sense within their religious tradition, of living with things which seem to challenge a particular interpretation of texts like the Bible. Indeed, Aquinas' adoption of Aristotle was radical in its day, and when he died his ideas were out of favour in the Church. One council in Paris (1277) even condemned the idea that Aristotle was compatible with Christianity. As argued in previous chapters, religion is always changing and adapting, and it has always taken on the world view of its day. As such, adapting to modern science is simply part of the tradition that makes up Christianity or any religion – just as Catholic Christianity rejected then embraced Ibn Sina's and Aquinas' Aristotelianism.

In discussions about the relationship of science and religion, various stances are often presented, first systematized by the scholar Ian Barbour. The first stance is that religion and science are in conflict. This is a common thesis propagated by many so-called New Atheists who see it as inherent, while many evangelical and fundamentalist Christians also take up this kind of stance today by advocating creationism or intelligent design. It is certainly not the norm historically (see Box 7.4). The second stance says that each can be seen as representing independent spheres, religion asking moral and spiritual questions, science talking about physical events. This has been popularized by a number of Christian and atheist scientists. Stephen Jay Gould promoted what he terms NOMA, or non-overlapping *magisteria* – that is, each has a separate area of authority and teachings. This also seems to have been Galileo's stance. It is perhaps a convenient belief, but one I see as problematic. The third stance is dialogue, where each engages the other. This, I believe, is inevitable, as splitting ethical and physical realms does not make sense. Contrary to the independence model, science and religion have areas where they rub up against each other. This can either be positive or negative. The final stance, Barbour suggested, was integration, where he himself ended up, which is that both would be seen as areas of knowledge in their own right, but offering complementary ways of knowing about the world. While many theologians have often been keen to endorse this, scientists have generally been less keen. For instance, the famous book *The Tao of Physics* (1975) by the renowned physicist Fritjof Capra was warmly welcomed by many Christians seeking rapprochement between the two fields, but it met with general indifference or even scorn by many fellow physicists.

To take one of these cases further, the argument has been made that while science can explain the universe, it cannot explain big metaphysical questions (e.g. Why is there something rather than nothing?). Of course, if there was nothing, there would be nobody to ask the question. Nevertheless, it holds out the possibility for those who wish for some form of spiritual belief or to argue that there must be something else, or at least that it cannot be disproven. Arguably, while Ockham's razor may have cut on God's side in the Middle Ages, it may go the other way today: Do we need this additional issue? Certainly, before Darwin, we had no way to explain how we had come here or how the complexity of creatures could exist: God was a useful hypothesis. After Darwin, another model exists. Perhaps it is an irony that this theological principle adopted by science may actually have an anti-religious side today. Even though, of course, it does not disprove God (no more than Ockham's usage 'proved' God); it merely suggests that it seems to be an unnecessary hypothesis. Of course, atheist critics have suggested that anything which cannot be disproved but is claimed without evidence can be simply dismissed without evidence; however, it is not clear that this viewpoint is so clear-cut. At the very least, religion is, for many, a culturally founded system that is embedded into their way of thinking, while as we discussed previously, there are arguments that being religious may be built into human nature through evolutionary patterns (see Chapters 1 and 8). If correct, this would suggest that religious people are not some special group who simply accept stories naively with no evidence for what they do, as the criticism suggests. Such a response is therefore simply unhelpful.

A more sophisticated argument to reject religion, which is that the nature of religion must be inimical to science, is made by Jerry Coyne. Religion is based on faith, science on reason; indeed, he sees any endeavour which is not based on science as essentially faulty and incapable of delivering any truth. He even sees academic disciplines like philosophy (which does not use empirical testing but only reason), pure maths (not empirical), history (unless it can use science) and the social sciences as also open to this criticism. Such a wide-ranging critique argued across several hundred pages would require a lengthy response to do it justice. However, first, 'faith'/'belief' is not a simple category only found in religion (see Chapter 1), and actually much of our life works on the basis of things we cannot test in the kind of ways Coyne demands; indeed, his arguments are reminiscent of the philosopher William Kingdom Clifford (1845–1879), who argued that only thoroughly tested beliefs were morally sound – an argument Clifford saw as destructive of religion. Thinkers since then have shown that his prescriptions are too demanding to be practical: we simply cannot live and act in the world if we have to stop and thoroughly examine, explore, research and fact-check every action, idea and opinion we have or wish to put into effect. Second, religion is not simply about faith but also uses reason and evidence in its support. Coyne suggests that religion only does this when it suits religion's agenda and rejects it when it does not; however, this claim is not factually based. Religions have often changed their attitudes in response to changing world views, and in the nineteenth century most Christians found no trouble adapting their thinking to accept evolution, just as seventeenth-century Protestants were happy to adopt a heliocentric world view. Third, Coyne cites many extreme cases of religious believers refusing to accept science (creationists and flat-earthers), refusing medical care (including cases of people allowing their children to die rather than use certain treatments) and similar cases, and he argues that any acceptance of 'faith' is the thin end of the wedge and that this is the inevitable result. However, his case is conjecture, and no direct correlation is shown. Certainly, in many countries where religion is strong, the extremes Coyne mentions would not be accepted. Indeed, his extreme dichotomy of science versus all other world views means that we would have to ban almost every opinion: political standpoints and affiliations are often adopted due to personal or family choices, and it is hard to say that any one can be shown to be demonstrably better by science; nationalism would likewise be disallowed because we could not show, scientifically, why any one country is superior or better than others – it would simply reflect an accident of birth. Again, his idea that because of extremes all religion is bad and anti-science would lead us to reject almost every culture known. Most cultures in the world have some elements which harm, oppress or marginalize others, and so presumably we must ban even seemingly harmless versions because they might allow us to have some tolerance for extremes in them.

While Coyne's arguments sound like sensible atheist polemics, they are not. Arguing only in favour of science can lead to truth and progress, so anything which isn't science is unsound and should not be allowed to influence how we live and think, is too extreme to have a practical application. It is also not an argument based in the scientific method: How does one make a hypothesis and test it empirically, as he demands? In other words, his argument that we must rely on, and trust in, science alone is not, and cannot be, backed up or supported by the scientific method he says is the only source of sure knowledge and truth. Furthermore, where would it leave us if he is right? While some like Sam Harris have suggested that science can help us develop morality, others, like Richard Dawkins, have argued that science of its very nature cannot do this. Clearly, there is not a single clear and objective scientific consensus on this, and again, given Coyne's very prescriptive rules for what counts as science, it is not clear how the scientific method could adjudicate. This may take us some way from the question of whether science and religion are always enemies, but – as with most ideas proposing an extreme – it cannot hold water on examination.

Even if one accepted that, today, religion and science are antithetical, it does not cut the feet out from underneath religion and spirituality altogether. As we discuss in Chapter 8, contemporary studies of neurology show that practices like meditation do have very real and beneficial effects on the human brain. In other words, religious practices do work (some of them at least; many others, of course, do not). Again, religion seems hardwired into the human DNA, meaning that it will not simply disappear. As such, remaining religious is not being impervious to the evidence; it is being naturally human. The evidence is far from conclusive either way: you can make a credible world view either with or without religion and develop a moral way of life from that basis. Like other arguments, Ockham's razor is more suggestive than offering certain proof; however, religious belief today needs to realize that scientific arguments, including evolution, make certain forms of belief more credible than others. While religious people need to see that others are quite justified in saying 'I have no need of that hypothesis', both standpoints offer credible ways of being human in today's world.

8

LIVING IN A RELIGIOUSLY DIVERSE, POST-CHRISTIAN AND POST-SECULAR WORLD

○ ○ ○

THE SCHOLARLY BIT

We have looked at many areas where religious and atheist spokespeople clash, and areas where both religious people and atheists disagree with their fellows. In this final chapter we will return to some familiar ground and also address new issues. I will suggest at least one meeting point, but not that there is simply *one* common set of things on which all can agree. But before that, let's address three areas of concern for contemporary living: first, the question of ethics and morality; second, whether religion will persist in society today and how it may continue to change; and third, making meaning, where we will look at issues like spirituality and rituals.

Ethics, God and no God

Ethical living, while an area where many agree, is also contested; on this ground, we see each side slinging mud at the other. While some atheists accuse religious people, variously, of needing an outdated book, having to fear divine punishments or desiring divine rewards to be moral (not to mention raising religion's moral record;

see Chapter 5), religious people have accused atheists of lacking morality or even being essentially immoral (see Box 8.1).

Box 8.1

Can you have morality without God?

While some religious polemics portray atheists as immoral and atheism as unable to ground a moral framework, there are many examples which show this is not true. These examples range from ancient philosophical thinkers in places like Greece and China (we discuss some examples in this chapter) to contemporary societies. For instance, in our contemporary world we do not see huge differences between religious and non-religious people in terms of their morality. While some psychological studies have shown that the belief you are being watched over (even by some unknown force) can make people less likely to perform some acts, such as taking things that are not theirs, conversely there has been a study showing that religious children are less moral. The latter case is far from conclusive, however, and must be balanced by other studies. All in all, though, other factors like relative wealth, background and social deprivation are all far more likely pointers towards moral behaviour and criminality than religious belief or its lack. Indeed, studies indicate that the wealthier someone perceives themselves to be, the less they respect others and the more likely they are to steal in certain situations. Meanwhile, social deprivation is linked to some forms of criminal behaviour. Notably, European countries with low levels of religious belief are not worse in terms of criminal behaviour and actually rank above many deeply religious countries in certain indicators of social cohesion, well-being and crime. Clearly, lack of belief in God does not make society fall apart nor people less moral to any significant degree.

Up until the Enlightenment, one of the chief arguments in favour of religion was that it was needed for morality: what would ground ethics if there was no God was the question that had to be answered. This is one reason why, during this period, the Buddha (c. fifth century BCE) and Confucius (c. 551–479 BCE) were extremely important for the foundations of atheism as alternatives to the prevailing Christian world view. Both were understood to be atheist philosophers (whether such a representation is accurate is another matter) who had created systems of morality that were seen to be at least the equal of Christianity. Therefore, it was argued, ethics could be underpinned without a divine mandate (although some Enlightenment atheists held that while atheism was suitable for themselves, it would not be suited to the common people who needed religion to keep them in line – hardly a progressive, enlightened attitude!). Such views accord with the Confucian atheist Xunzi (third century BCE) who argued that while rites and rituals had no supernatural quality, they were nevertheless essential to keep society in check (see Box 8.6). Since that time, ideas have moved on. While Europe, today, is exceptional in the high degree of atheism found there, it provides evidence that atheists are capable of living morally and harmoniously based upon their world view (see Box 8.1 and below). Moreover, two famous atheist theorists dealt important blows to ideas of religious morality. One of them was Karl Marx (1818–1883) who argued, with considerable force, that religion actually served the desires of the ruling classes. By telling the working masses that their 'reward' would come in a future world, current inequality wasn't challenged. Religion, far from being the source of morality, was actually, in the Marxist critique, the inequitable imposition of the will of the ruling class on society and so essentially immoral. As the 'opium of the people' religion was a source of injustice and oppression. Of course, religion has also been used to justify rebellion and social action against the existing order. In the Liberation Theology that developed in Latin America in the 1970s, Marxism was used by Christians to return to themes advocating what was seen as the biblical 'option for the poor'. Certainly, many scholars would argue that such a reading is more in accord with the historical Jesus than the institutionalized support of inequality and the kind of Prosperity Gospel that has now spread globally (often inspired by right-wing American evangelicals and opportunist Pentecostal preachers, who grow rich upon the faith of their often impoverished flock). As such, while not endorsing the Marxist critique as true of all religion, it is clear that both historically and today that religion has been used to justify oppression and make religious leaders wealthy.

Friedrich Nietzsche (1844–1900) had a somewhat different argument, and while often seen alongside Marx amongst the so-called masters of suspicion (i.e. Marx, Nietzsche and Freud) who led to the undermining of religion, their views are actually potentially in conflict. Nietzsche's argument was that originating amongst the poor, slaves and other underclasses, Christianity has, in fact, enacted a huge revolution whereby what he termed slave morality triumphed over an aristocratic warrior morality. In other words, ideals of mercy, compassion and equality (qualities that slaves and the oppressed would value) had dominated over the older order of warrior rulers who prized bravery, acknowledging self-worth (as opposed to undue humility) and strength. For Nietzsche, therefore, being atheist didn't mean simply being good and disbelieving in God; this, he thought, was easy as one could comfortably maintain one's old Christian indoctrination as to what was right and wrong. Rather, he suggested, the atheist should overcome conventional morality and become a 'superman' (*Übermensch*). Whether Nietzsche's descent into madness is attributable to his trying to live beyond compassion and love is debatable, but this is certainly not a critique of atheism as a whole. Nietzsche's historical analysis was also very dubious and driven by his ideology rather than seeking to uncover the evidence. Nevertheless, he raises important questions about the way that we seek to found our moral systems and what ideals we value. We may expect, perhaps, atheist morality to look somewhat different from Christian morality; remembering of course that every Christian tradition, if not individual, has a different moral system. (Even a set of fairly standard rules or injunctions like the Ten Commandments or the Beatitudes from the Gospels are interpreted and lived out differently.) Nietzsche's more general point, picked up by existential philosophers like Jean-Paul Sartre (1905–1980) and Simone de Beauvoir (1908–1986), suggest that it is possible to look to different moral values, or that moral values can be accessed from non-Christian (or non-religious) sources especially in terms of what it means to live an authentic human life.

Nietzsche's ideas on Christian morality are mainly of historical interest, although Marx's critique has had more lasting impact. While the supposedly Communist states have largely disappeared or become capitalist, the structural point that Marx made about the way that religion can become an instrument of oppression remains pertinent (see Box 8.2). Through the legacy of figures like Sigmund Freud (1856–1939) we have become aware of more internal ways that values and world views influence our subconscious. Although Freud's own system was surely faulty, psychology has become very important in understanding people's morality and world views. All of this provides resources for both religious and atheist people to understand these issues today. (We come back to ethical questions in the concluding section of this chapter, so we'll leave this discussion for the moment.)

Box 8.2

> ### The Christian dialogue with Marxism
> While the collapse of the European Communist states and China's adaptation of capitalism has seen Marxism drop off most people's agenda, for a considerable part of the late twentieth-century Marxism or Communism was one of the most prominent world views that had to be debated. Indeed, when the World Council of Churches (the most significant global Christian interdenominational organization) founded its structures on interreligious dialogue it included, within this, dialogue with world views such as Marxism as one strand. Many papers, books and meetings during the 1970s–1980s explored the Christian–Marxist dialogue.

Religions in society today

Daniel Dennett suggested that we have five options for the future, which I rephrase below:

- *The secularization thesis* holds that religion will die out, but this seems wrong: religion is here to stay and appears resurgent, so we have to accept this.

- *Religion's death throes* implies the upsurge against secularization is actually the last gasp; in future, at most, we'll see a ceremonial vestige.

- *Transformation* indicates that new spiritual self-help organizations will arise, creating rituals and traditions to maintain numbers.

- *Religion sidelined* means that it becomes socially marginal and regarded as morally deficient; while not banned, adults may choose it as a vice, and it isn't taught to children (just as we wouldn't let them drink alcohol) to avoid 'corrupting' them.

- *The end of the world arrives* implies that whichever religion got it right is proved correct as their followers are saved and others damned. (Following some interpretations actually everyone is saved, or maybe everyone is proved wrong.)

Whether the fifth item is ironic or simply an unfalsifiable philosophical probability is not clear. It also shows the rather Western bias of Dennett's categories and perceptions; most Buddhists, for instance, expect no end times: the universe simply continues and in due course a new Buddha will arrive and teach the *dharma* again. While Dennett's five categories don't outline every option, and possibly some combinations are possible, it raises the question: What do we think will happen?

Developing a theme from Chapter 1, some evolutionary biologists argue that religion could be part of being human. Let's take this starting point: If religion is false, why would this be? Certain forms of behaviour are useful, and one of them is finding patterns and meaningful connections. When faced with a predator, being able to associate the pattern of stripes in the grass with a sabre-toothed feline means you can run away; indeed, the person who does this better, which may include running away from a number of imaginary tigers, bears, snakes or whatever it may be, will be the one who lives. The person who is not so good, while not being fooled by the wrongful associations, may also miss the predator: it only makes one mistake to get eaten. Some mistakes are more evolutionary beneficial than others. Likewise, we form other (imaginary) associations. The finding of religiously meaningful shapes or faces in naturally occurring phenomena is an example of the way we are conditioned to identify faces and make connections. It is not a crazy thing religious people do, but rather a normal human impulse to make patterns in data (though for a scientifically educated person to mistake a pattern of seeds in a melon for a revelation may seem crazy). Likewise, it seems a general cultural pattern to associate consciousness to the dead; humans are not alone in treating our dead in ceremonial ways (it is reportedly recorded amongst some other primates), as such behaviour is also found in elephants. There are reasons given for this in terms of the way we expect consciousness and relations to exist. Again, children creating imaginary friends has also been interpreted to show that fairly normal (i.e. non-supernatural) evolutionary, explainable behaviour may be behind such phenomena. Both this and the human tendency to associate consciousness to the dead may therefore provide evidence of the way that beliefs in some transcendent reality develop in ways we can term 'natural'. In other words, normal human patterns of meaning making and association may lead us to develop beliefs in some form of transcendence, which may be a by-product of various evolutionary useful or explainable behaviours.

The evidence that religion is simply an evolutionary by-product is far from proven with counterarguments existing. Nevertheless, much of the argument has a high degree of plausibility, but even if certain aspects of religion can be explained this way, the complexity and diversity of the phenomenon we label 'religion' would not show that this explained all religion, nor that it disproved it directly.

I won't extend this debate here, but rather take us in another direction. If religion is hardwired into us (an idea many religious people would agree with, even if for other reasons), we would expect religion to continue to exist. The fact that religion has returned, even resurgent, after many decades of atheist teaching and rule in places like Russia and China, is again evidence of the strong human inclination to it. During the Cultural Revolution in China (1966–1976) many scholars concluded that Chinese folk religion and Daoism had been obliterated. Today, however, between them they seemingly count for most of the religiosity in China, notwithstanding that atheist numbers remain high. Interestingly, a cross-university research project that began some time ago in the UK exploring levels of reported 'spiritual experience' was extended into both Turkey and mainland China. A research hypothesis was that China would show lower levels of such reporting, while Turkey may potentially outstrip the UK. In actuality, though, it was remarkable that almost universal levels of 'spiritual experience' were reported across these three nations. Notably, care was taken to translate the questions using native scholars and trials were taken to sample the questionnaires and eliminate other possible bias factors. (Words often used to translate 'religion' or 'spiritual' carry different connotations across the three countries; such factors explain why different surveys in Japan have suggested that levels of 'religious belief/belonging' vary from virtually none to extremely high; indeed, one of the best estimates suggests the average Japanese person believes/belongs/identifies with 2.8 religions). Other studies, which are usefully and accessibly discussed by the atheist thinker Dylan Evans, suggest that levels of dopamine in the brain may be indicative of the chances of having religious experiences. I find the interpretation of this rather problematic, because it makes an assumption that religious experience is one type of thing, whereas studies across traditions suggest very different forms of experiences. Nevertheless, it does suggest that certain forms of experience associated with religion are related to chemical impulses. It is not clear, though, what this tells us (see Box 8.3).

Box 8.3

Confirmation bias

Neuroscientist Andrew Newberg has studied responses to his discovery that religious experiences of nuns were detectable in the brain. Atheists considered it proof that religious experience was simply a brain state. The nuns, however, made sense of it another way: their whole being was involved in encountering God, including the brain/body and not just the spirit/soul, which delighted them. Coyne argues that when religious people find evidence that doesn't fit their world view, they *make* it fit. This is confirmation bias, which means using new evidence to back up your already existing world view. However, as Newberg argues, this is not some special facility of people we label religious. Everybody, including atheists, do it. He argues that his studies do not support either position: the atheists and nuns simply employ confirmation bias to support existing beliefs. Of course, confirmation bias is not always a bad thing: if we changed our ideas radically every time a potentially new piece of information came along, we would have no fixed ideas. For good practical reasons of understanding and logic, we try to make sense of new evidence in terms of what we already know, what the philosopher Hans-Georg Gadamer (1900–2002) would call 'prejudice'. Gadamer argued that we should not see this in negative terms, as we can only understand anything because we have existing ideas. However, it becomes a logical fallacy when we fail to see that a new piece of evidence requires us to rethink our existing world view or prejudices. Indeed, I find that a lot of the 'New Atheist literature' (on both sides) is essentially about confirmation bias: each side simply fits evidence into their world view, ignoring, obscuring or falsely claiming ambiguous data.

We have reviewed quite a bit of evidence and various examples here, so what does it mean? I am going to get somewhat speculative here: religion is something that human beings do naturally; by this word I mean it is a 'normal' (due to evolution, culture, society, divine creation or whatever) behaviour which can be interpreted materialistically or religiously depending on your standpoint. The tendency to experience something that we would understand as beyond the normal phenomenal course of the world is intrinsic (chemically, evolutionarily, spiritually – take your pick). As such, we really should not expect religion to die out, at least not any time soon. A widening of religious options and the possibility of being atheist (without repression) are likely to become the norm across more of the world. However, for reasons of upbringing, inbuilt tendencies, spiritual yearnings or whatever else, I would expect some form of religious/spiritual belief, identity and/or belonging to remain the norm. I will even go out on a limb here and suggest that this will occur in around 60–65% of people for the foreseeable future. Atheism, too, is likely to peak around 15–25%. 'Floaters' – agnostics and those hard to categorize – will also continue to exist. Importantly, though, I expect conventional belonging to major religions to decline. This applies primarily to the West; different dynamics probably make institutional belonging more common elsewhere due to varied social and cultural factors in terms of the way traditions and societies operate. These figures may change in the long term, but I feel confident in this prediction over the next few decades, and maybe to the end of the century.

Let's answer some potential queries. First, if there is an evolutionary basis for religion, we should not expect to see huge and immediate changes. It may happen over time that those who may be more inclined to make the connections we spoke of above become less significant – that is, in the modern world being able to spot tigers in the undergrowth is not the evolutionary advantage it used to be! Second, if factors are more complex (I strongly suspect so), we will see social, cultural and other changes being more dominant than the biological ones, which means that what we see as normal or acceptable will adjust as society adjusts. I also suspect that having an inbuilt spiritual awareness or propensity may have other advantages, for example, social networks, mental well-being (discussed below) and so forth.

Before leaving this topic, let's also address how we may expect religion to change. I mentioned that a survey of Japan showing people having an average of 2.8 religions, which from a Christian or Muslim (Abrahamic monotheistic) model may seem nonsensical. However, the Far East does religion differently. It is less about accepting beliefs or doctrines as the sole basis of your religion; rather, you will go to whichever temple is convenient or has the reputation for specific roles: in both China and Japan, people have looked to Buddhist monks for funerals; in China, people traditionally want a Celestial Master lineage Daoist to perform exorcisms, but found Confucianism providing the basis for communal morality; in Japan it is often said that you're born Shinto, marry Christian and die Buddhist. Such picking and choosing, or even multiple belonging, is normal in many parts of Asia and is becoming more common in the West too (see Box 8.4).

Box 8.4

Multiple religious belonging/identity
Many people practise as Buddhist–Christians, that is, they perform rituals and practices associated with both religions. Some people see themselves as predominantly a member of one but draw so heavily from the other that they cannot say they belong to one alone. Some identify almost equally with both and may well be initiated members of each. For Judaism, a term Jubu has been created for those Jews who use Buddhist meditation or identify with it strongly as their spiritual path, while still keeping a Jewish ceremonial identity. While multiple, or dual, identities often involve Buddhism, it is not limited to this, and Christian–Pagan, Australian Aboriginal Muslims and other multiple identities exist.

Two British scholars, Linda Woodhead and Paul Heelas, have argued that we were seeing a spiritual revolution whereby people are leaving traditional organized religious communities for more diffuse 'spiritual' practices like yoga, meditation or wider networks where they find spiritual meaning. While the methodology of their study has been strongly criticized, many feel that there is circumstantial evidence that suggests something similar. Certainly across much of the Western world, it is no longer simply Christianity – or even just Judaism and

Islam – that provides the religious options. An increasing number identify by terms such as 'spiritual but not religious'. Others are categorized as 'nones' in census date, meaning they do not identify with any single religion, but it has been found that they veer to spirituality of some form. Whether this is seen as 'religious' may be debatable if you define religion as having a God. While some (both religious and atheist) wish to draw strict borders, atheism and some forms of spiritual practice are not always distinct. Indeed, such forms of 'spirituality' (see Box 4.3) may become more of an established norm, including such things as yoga, meditation, revived Pagan festivals and practices, elements of Christianity or other traditions like Judaism or Islam, and an infusion of ideas from contemporary society. On this last item, while some people write Jedi (of *Star Wars* fame) on census and questionnaires of religious identity as a joke, there are established and serious 'churches' of Jedism and people who follow it as their spiritual discipline. For scholars of religion, such new community formation is utterly fascinating; don't forget that most new religions seemed pretty bizarre to the society around them when they were new or young – one only has to read what some Romans had to say about the Christians for an example: for instance, one Roman critic suggested that Christians ate babies smothered in flour (misunderstanding the imagery of eating Jesus' body and blood in the Eucharistic ceremony); another accused followers of conducting secret sexual orgies (a misunderstanding of the symbolism and practice of baptism, which used to be done with new converts stripping to show a leaving behind of their old life before donning white clothing as a sign of a new purity).

Spirituality, meaning and rituals

Spirituality is an extremely contested term amongst atheists: some see it as associated with religion and supernatural, and so is to be rejected; others see it as a necessity in some new form. This very much intersects with what we have just been saying, so let's take our discussion in a different direction by invoking the word 'meaning'.

Stereotypes may suggest that religious believers have a meaning determined and given by some external authority or text, while atheists build their own meaning through reason. However, things are rarely so neat or simple. First, the idea that all religions teach just one path or that everyone within them understands it the same way is far too simplistic. Religious people (again, we have asked what this really means) have to build their own meaning from the society, community and religious choices available. Of course, for many this meaning will be constructed as much through family, jobs or personal goals and interests as through their belief or faith. Likewise, atheists may read other atheists' books and construct an identity or meaning based on this, or else will find family, jobs, sports or spirituality in some form as determinative. Figures like Marx, Nietzsche, Sartre and Beauvoir have been inspirational for many, but also figures like Darwin and Dawkins help shape people's world views.

It may be suggested, though, that at some 'higher' level, religious belief gives a universe which is directed or purposeful in some way, whereas the atheist universe is essentially just random molecules without an ultimate meaning. Few people, of course, build their lives by relating to 'ultimate realities'; rather, we relate to the more mundane world around us. I am not convinced, therefore, that we really see a huge difference: atheist Humanists may see value inherent to each unique individual, and so helping them to personal fulfilment provides meaning; but religious people may equally gain meaning by doing good in the here and now, where we exist primarily in relation to our fellow humans, other creatures (important for many Buddhists, Pagans and increasingly Christians), or the whole ecology of our planet. Meaning is more often than not located in the local. (As I will discuss below, in practical ways, both religious belief and atheism may find common ground in practice and ethical living; ideas on exactly what this is may differ, but certain similar goals or ends may exist.) Focusing here and now, rather than on abstract concepts, may be useful in a world where people of all religions and none need to coexist.

This question of the local will bring us very briefly to discuss rituals. Throughout human history, societies have often made sense of what they are and how those within them relate to each other through various communal rites, a matter classically analysed by Émile Durkheim (1858–1917). In a world where we often lack shared religious or communal identities, it is unclear where we would look for them. This in part lies behind the development of what are often termed 'atheist churches' and is explored by Alain de Botton (see Chapter 4). Whatever source we look to, as part of human communities we may need some form of modes of interacting which connect us. These can be grand national (or international) events or simple everyday courtesies like wishing people good day. Whatever form they take, though, religions have often underpinned our collective rituals and sense of belonging (like saying 'bless you' when someone sneezes). In a world that is more diverse, where we lack a sense of common community or identity, we may ask what rites connect people. It is not my intention to suggest how we could build new rituals or forms of communicating (although Robert Neville Cummings, an American Confucian scholar, has suggested that this could be one contribution of the Confucian tradition to global culture in our contemporary age). The question, however, needs to be raised in relation to increasingly diverse societies where such diversity will increasingly become normative. In civil society, citizens and communities need to think about issues like democracy, human rights, deliberation on the common good and how we communicate in the public sphere. This relates both to individual and collective questions of meaning and coexistence.

WHAT CAN CHRISTIANS, ATHEISTS AND OTHERS SHARE TODAY?

The final heading may seem very ambitious, and I do not want to suggest some nice or simple meeting place; however, I will move in a personal way in this direction. I say 'personal' because these will very much be my own thoughts, and I suspect that my community of readers will surely want to debate, argue and discuss what I have put forward. To this end, I begin discussing what we have said above about morality. If we are concerned with living together today – accepting as I have suggested that people holding traditional religious identities, new religious identities and atheist identities will coexist for a long time to come – we need to think about what standards we can hold in common. I will do this by invoking one thing which may be shared, which is the idea of compassion. Indeed, I will suggest that we can all see ourselves living in a universe where compassion should drive us.

Compassion

To speak of the universe as a place of compassion may seem to invoke unnecessarily religious or spiritual conceptions; however, I believe it proves a place where atheists, Christians, adherents of other religions and those with no religion may meet. Many atheists, and rightly so, will insist that they do not need any higher power to ground their morality, to tell right from wrong, to lead good and noble lives. Clearly, this is so, as the Confucian philosopher Mencius (c. 372–289 CE) tells us the innate human instinct of hearing a child stuck in a well impels in all but the most corrupt minds an instantaneous desire to help. (See the discussion on natural law in Chapter 1.) Compassion is, to some extent at least, hardwired into (most of) us.

Let's imagine three narratives to explain this. First, we could put it down to socialization. As creatures within communities and families we learn from an early age, as children on their mother's breast, that giving, love and tenderness are necessary components of our survival. Society is inherently social and therefore inherently compassionate: to be a human animal is to be a social animal, a compassionate animal. Of course, this may be seen beyond the human world (for instance, stories of dolphins rescuing drowning humans may be indicative of this).

Second, we could take a step back and speak about evolution as a driving force in making us compassionate; to survive we need others, and so our species instinct is to develop bonds of compassion. Perhaps, therefore, even pre-socially, we may be hardwired to be social and compassionate. As humans, we have a capacity born through generations of breeding to develop these traits. I suspect it would be mighty hard to prove such an assertion genetically, but it may well be so, just as we have brains pre-programmed to develop language and other skills.

Third, here I'm taking a further leap, but if survival is evolutionarily geared towards rewarding compassion, at least amongst certain species (certainly more complex or highly developed organisms), is it too far to say that something in the universe favours compassion? Of course, bare matter may not care whether anything evolves or not. In the many millions, billions even, of universes that we may speculate have existed, it may well be that no other significant life has evolved. (Of course, we have no way of knowing, but is our universe the norm or the exception?) However, in any universe where evolution does take place, it does not seem far-fetched to assume, or argue, that in terms of evolution (and therefore from a humanistic point of view) compassion is rewarded; therefore, the universe has a principle that makes compassion, from that perspective, a universal value – maybe not an absolute value for the universe, but a universal and humanistic value.

Clearly, we could take a fourth step and claim that compassion is built into, favoured or inherent within the universe. I suspect that many religiously inclined people would veer that way (and obviously it could be seen as an upshot of the argument) and this is perhaps a reason why the atheist will resist it. However, I do not think it has to be rejected on these grounds, and certainly it is not a simple argument for a theistic answer, as may be assumed from somebody from a Christian context. On the night Siddhartha Gautama, the Buddha (c. fifth century BCE), had his awakening experience, it is recorded that as he came to his recognition about the nature of the universe (the beliefs of our reincarnation and immersion within patterns of anger, ignorance and desire), he became more compassionate. This, in both the Theravada and Mahayana traditions, is innate in the state of Buddhahood; indeed, the pattern he set out to escape the cycle of reincarnation also inherently favours compassion (*karuna* or *metta*, though the latter is often translated as 'loving kindness') – from a Buddhist world view, not because of God but just because of the way the universe is! Moreover, as we have suggested, various non-theistic traditions, like Buddhism and Confucianism, can see compassion as inherent in the universe for reasons of its very nature (notwithstanding, especially in a figure like Xunzi in Confucianism, some potential countertrends). Furthermore, I would also suggest that it can be seen as compatible with a humanistic world view. My argument above that various arguments for seeing being humans in an evolutionary perspective as involving compassion could work in the same direction. I don't wish to argue that humanists, or atheists, need such an argument to secure their ethical foundations, but I believe it wouldn't harm, and as I've suggested, it may help make connections with religious figures. This may help open avenues of dialogue, communication and mutual understanding, not just between atheists, Christians and Muslims, but also between non-theistic systems such as Buddhism or Confucianism.

Box 8.5

A global ethic?

At the 1993 World Parliament of Religions, the Swiss theologian Hans Küng proposed a new ethical code which he thought everyone could accept: the Global Ethic. It had four main pillars: 1) non-violence and respect for life; 2) solidarity and a just economic order; 3) tolerance and a life of truthfulness; and 4) equal rights and partnership between men and women. While quite a few of the religious leaders signed the document, many did not. While Küng's proposals may seem like common ideas, there were disagreements. For instance, in item 1, does 'non-violence' mean complete pacifism or is self-defence and a 'just war' allowed, a matter on which religions disagree. Meanwhile, in item 4, for some conservative members within certain religions, they opposed the language of equal rights because they saw it in Western and secular terms; in their world view, men and women may be spirituality equal, but they have different spheres of operation, the former the public sphere, the latter the domestic sphere (see Chapter 6). These four basics therefore proved to be too contentious or simply so generic that actual practice and understanding was impossible. Scholars have therefore argued that rather than seeking a single common global ethic, it is better to move towards progressive moral and ethical values within the culturally specific terms of each religion.

One argument that may still arise is over what is meant by our term 'compassion', and certainly it is far from clear that Buddhist terms like *metta* (loving kindness) or *karuna* (compassion), Christian terms like *agape* (love) or *caritas* (charity or compassion) or secular usages of compassion or kindness all mean identical things; indeed, advocates of each system will often level charges at the others of their failures in this regard. We need not cite examples here as I assume we can all imagine or remember such accusations. Nevertheless, I do not see this as a compelling or final argument. There may not be a single common ethic, but we can share many moral values and behaviours (see Box 8.5). Let's not forget that disagreements occur within one tradition (see Box 8.6). While such concepts have quite different usages (e.g. Does it apply only (or primarily) to humans or all animals? Are families or wider society the principle recipients? Is ethical behaviour letting others follow their own path or actively seeking their conversion?). Clearly, what Jesus' early disciples meant by *agape*, what medieval Sri Lankan Buddhists meant by *metta* or contemporary atheists mean by 'compassion' are distinct; however, equally all agree on certain actions, and Mencius' example of the child in the well exemplifies this.

Box 8.6

Are humans good or evil? A Confucian debate

A famous dispute in the classical Confucian tradition concerns two contrasting perspectives on human nature, represented by Mencius and Xunzi. Mencius believed that human nature was inherently good, and that only through interaction with the human world do we become bad. He told a story of Ox Mountain. Imagine a beautiful wooded mountain covered in trees; however, people in the surrounding neighbourhood wanted wood, and so they went there and chopped the trees down. Over time, people visiting Ox Mountain just came to see a barren and ugly wasteland; however, we must remember its original nature, Mencius tells us. This he takes as an analogy of wicked people who have been corrupted such that they forget what they were once like, or could have been. Xunzi saw human nature as inherently corrupt, and argued that rituals and society's rules were needed to keep us in check. Therefore, only the correct training can make us noble and good, and even become, eventually, a sage.

Most traditions have some debate of this kind, and I mention it as a point of contestation that needs to be considered before I suggest that we naively see compassion as underlying human society and nature. I think we need a more nuanced story that takes both sides into account, but I would not see this as going against what I have said. Certainly we will all take different positions on this; nevertheless, whatever stance we take, at a bottom line, we can find some unity in diverse notions of compassion: treating others with respect, caring for those in need and expressing kindness as a basic way of interacting.

Adaptation and dialogue

We conclude by drawing out some themes discussed above alongside some final points. First, we need to accept that all traditions change over time, whether this be atheism or a religious tradition. Simplistic notions that religions do one type of thing, or the kind of monolithic comments such as 'all religion is bad', 'the essence of all religion is peace' and so forth, are simply naive. Equally, if atheism is seen as simply one homogenous thing, we misconstrue it and neglect its divergent trends, rationales and manifestations. This, of course, means that those within these traditions need to think about what they are and how they can develop today. Of course, some religious people will object: their tradition is a once-and-for-all final revelation given inerrantly that expresses everything about what can be said and known. These people, as I have argued, do not know the history of their tradition, and certainly for many traditions there are good internal (theological) reasons for rejecting such a narrative. It suggests they have a very limited and simplistic God who is readily encapsulated in human words. (That, however, is an argument every religion needs to have internally.) Liberal traditions which hard-line believers and many atheist critics deride as 'watering down' religion, 'not true to tradition' or simply 'accommodating' to science or secularism can actually make more coherent sense of the history of their tradition and their place within it than most traditionalist, fundamentalist or conservative variations. By arguing that religions are culturally and historically derived and changeable, they acknowledge the actual dynamics of the history of religions. The German theologian Paul Tillich (1886–1965) advanced what he called a Theology of Correlation in which religious concerns are related to modern ways of thinking, in his case existential philosophy. He argued, though, that although he had named a new method, it is what theology and religion had always done.

In every age religion adapts itself to the prevailing world view and expresses itself in those terms. For instance, in the early Christian centuries, figures like Augustine of Hippo (354–430) expressed Christianity in terms of neo-Platonic philosophy, in the Middle Ages Thomas Aquinas (1225–1274) used the fashionable new Aristotelian philosophy, in the Enlightenment period figures like William Paley (1743–1805) used a new Natural Theology, as they called it – whereas religious conservatives, and some atheists, say that religion is fixed, which often leads to incoherence by denying the actual interrelations of history, science or other things with religion. Liberal or progressive theologies are in accord with the way religions have always adapted to changing cultural and scientific world views. The history of religions shows us that this is the constant pattern.

Another issue is whether there is any clear common ground where each camp can meet. I have sketched out some personal views above, but even within each tradition people cannot agree: atheists disagree as to whether religion is an evil to be opposed or a useful resource to be mined; every religion argues over everything from doctrine, to ethics, to social policy, to organizational structures. Amongst all traditions, though, I believe there are resources which say that we can and should respect other viewpoints and recognize the truths that everybody finds and can give respect to their honest search for truth and meaning. Such resources and viewpoints are often not those given prominence; indeed, it is a factor that social psychologists have identified in the way we construct our own identities that we overemphasize in-group and out-group markers to more clearly make certain people different from us and our in-group. This is not simply a religious function, of course, but occurs in politics, sports, gender and almost every other area where human beings construct identities. Nevertheless, I believe it is no reason not to create narratives which promote agreement and which can in turn lead to dialogue and greater understanding (see Box 8.7). This book, indeed, is offered as one step in a dialogue between what are often seen as two opposed groups: the religious and the atheists. While each group can demonize and vilify the other, this situation is neither natural nor necessary.

Box 8.7

Interreligious dialogue

In 1893, a landmark event, the Parliament of the World's Religions, held in conjunction with a Chicago World Trade Fair, saw representatives from many religions given equal space and time to speak about their tradition. Conducted in a spirit of mutual understanding and respect, rather than antagonism or judgement, it was the most representative dialogical event the world had ever seen. Though far from ideal, it gave rise to a movement and organizations which have seen dialogue grow from a fringe interest in religions to being one of the primary modes of engagement between them. Both the Catholic Church and the World Council of Churches, and many individual Protestant and Orthodox Churches, have departments for dialogue, and this is encouraged both formally and is conducted at grassroots levels. As mentioned in Box 8.2, the dialogue with certain atheist world views has been a part of this, and increasingly humanists and atheists are included. Some interreligious organizations deal only with specifically named religions and so often atheists are not included or invited to discussions, although some have included them on their list of groups covered. Elsewhere, often in informal ways, atheist groups or individuals do become part of dialogical exchanges either with specific people, groups or religious traditions. Notably, since 9/11 especially, interest in interreligious dialogue has moved beyond simply religious communities to become encouraged by governments, civil society and wider communities.

A final issue to mention is that whichever way the debate is discussed, there will always be cultural and personal differences between people. The kind of dialogue I advocate would not be the way everyone wants to proceed. For instance, the current Western context sees religious–atheist polemic as the norm. This reflects one strand from the Enlightenment legacy, but it is not the only way to understand the heritage of the Enlightenment, nor is it a necessary global norm. A Chinese atheist may find Xunzi more significant for their understanding than Voltaire (1694–1778), Charles Darwin (1809–1882) or Christopher Hitchens (1949–2011). Likewise, in a predominantly Buddhist culture, especially in a Theravada context where the Buddha is understood as a human being who taught the way to awakening, rather than any form of deity, this may set up the debate between religious people and atheists very differently, as the conversation would have different presuppositions. In our increasingly globalized world, we will all need to learn from different cultures. Furthermore, both religion and atheism need to recognize that they have often had colonial or imperialist aspects or presumptions; Western (i.e. European–American) norms, models and values have taken centre stage or been seen as normative. Contemporary discussions need to be aware of this.

I conclude by saying that what I have offered here is very much a personal reflection, although in terms of my intention to offer the resources for 'better disagreement' I have it set out based on what I believe is a fact-based academic account. The book overall has tried to show how debates have evolved, what situations really are and how arguments on both sides have been misrepresented and misconstrued. Nevertheless, other people would have asked different questions, addressed different topics and, in some cases where it is an issue of interpretation rather than simply a case of presenting clear and straightforward facts (some would argue that there are no simple facts and everything is interpretation), they would have interpreted differently. However, this is part of debate and dialogue, and if different opinions and arguments are not brought to the table, then there can be no forward movement. If I have contributed towards such a dialogue, I will be happy.

FURTHER READING

I have tried to cite accessible and readily available sources for further reading; however, in some cases, more academic or obscure texts are noted. Most sources will also take you to further writings and discussions. The sources here are not a comprehensive reference for every idea or point made, simply suggestions to some useful or interesting extra sources. I apologize for citing a number of my own works and from texts I have edited; this is done where I have, or the authors cited have, specific subject expertise and discuss arguments in accessible ways (i.e. my more obscure academic tracts are not referenced). Dates for books reflect either first publication or latest editions, but other editions and dates may also exist for many titles. I do not include texts already cited in the main text.

SETTING THE DEBATES IN CONTEXT (CHAPTER 1)

One context for this book involves the writers often termed the 'New Atheists' (such as Richard Dawkins, Sam Harris, Christopher Hitchens and Daniel Dennett). On the whole, I am not writing in response to them and do not list their books here, as they are well known. I have also used online interviews or talks, often from YouTube, to understand their ideas, including for figures like Laurence Krauss. I do specifically take issue with Jerry Coyne, and his work is cited in the text. This is because his is one of the latest texts of this type, and he has tried to engage religious texts and thinkers more than many others. While I do not respond explicitly to every point he makes, it has helped me shape parts of this book and phrase it more carefully.

On criticisms of the New Atheism stance, see Michael Shermer, 'Atheism and Liberty', in Alex Bentley, ed., *The Edge of Reason?* (2008)

– a very good book which I cite often – and amongst the best religious responses is Alister McGrath, *Dawkins' God* (2005). An overview is Ian S. Markham and Christine Faulstich, 'The New Atheists', in Paul Hedges, ed., *Controversies in Contemporary Religion*, vol. 2 (2014). On a related theme about the concept of 'scientism', see John Lennox, 'Scientific Fundamentalism', in James D.G. Dunn, ed., *Fundamentalism: Threats and Ideologies in the Modern World* (2016).

I could not list all my sources for discussing atheism and religion, so simply note some useful ones. For atheism: Michael Ruse, *Atheism: What Everyone Needs to Know* (2015); Michael Ruse, ed., *The Oxford Handbook of Atheism* (2013) (especially for this chapter the essays by Ariela Keysar and Juhem Navarro-Rivera, Callum Brown, Alan Kors and Graham Oppy); and Dylan Evans, *Atheism* (2014). For religion: publishers like Routledge, Oxford University Press, I.B. Tauris and Cambridge University Press have good introductions to religious traditions.

On 'religion' as a problematic term, see Anna King and Paul Hedges, 'What is Religion? Or, What Is It We Are Talking About?' in Hedges, *Controversies in Contemporary Religion*, vol. 1. Notably, some critics will suggest the term should be abandoned; however, I have retained it here, because I believe it can be usefully and viably employed, an explanation and rationale for which is provided in the chapter cited and in further works referenced therein.

On religion's potentially evolutionary basis, Pascal Boyer, *Religion Explained: The Evolutionary Origins of Religious Thought* (2002) is a classic. Balanced essays and discussion are found in Bentley, *The Edge of Reason?* (especially Lewis Wolpert, 'The evolution of religion'; Steven Mithen, 'Is religion inevitable? An archaeologist's view'). For a counter to such arguments from a religious perspective, see Neil Messer, *Selfish Genes and Christian Ethics* (2007).

For surveys on science and religion, see www.pewforum. org/2009/11/05/scientists-and-belief; http://phys.org/news/2015-12-worldwide-survey-religion-science-scientists.html; http://ns.umich. edu/new/releases/7256-study-shows-how-college-major-and-religious-faith-affect-each-other. This is also discussed in various chapters in Bentley, *The Edge of Reason?*

On identity and religion, see Paul Hedges and Angela Coco, 'Belonging, Behaving, Believing, Becoming: Religion and Identity' in Hedges, *Controversies in Contemporary Religion*, vol. I.

BOOKS AND BELIEFS: CHOOSING AND INTERPRETING TEXTS (CHAPTER 2)

On the compilation of the biblical canon, see John Barton, *How the Bible Came to Be* (1997). For some history on Christianity's development, see Linda Woodhead, *An Introduction to Christianity* (2004). Other good books on the collection and understanding of Christian scripture include Bart Ehrman, *The New Testament: A Historical Introduction to the Early Christian Writings* (2012). On Buddhism's scriptures, see Cathy Cantwell, *Buddhism: The Basics* (2010), Chapter 3; on the Qur'an, see Michael Cook, *The Koran: A Very Short Introduction* (2000).

On the concept of Fundamentalism, see Christopher J. van der Krogt, 'The Rise of Fundamentalisms', in Hedges, *Controversies in Contemporary Religion*, vol. 3.

On Tillich's Theology of Correlation, see the article on him in the *Boston Collaborative Encyclopaedia of Western Theology*, http://people.bu.edu/wwildman/bce/tillich.htm.

AUTHORITY FIGURES: JESUS AND THE OTHERS (CHAPTER 3)

An excellent comparative survey of Jesus, the Buddha and Muhammad is Paul Gwynne, *Buddha, Jesus and Muhammad* (2014).

On religious authority, see Paul Hedges and Christina Welch, 'Charisma, Scriptures, Revelation, and Reason: Sources of Religious Authority' in Hedges, *Controversies in Contemporary Religion*, vol. 1.

On the Buddha, most introductions cover this, and authors to look for include Peter Harvey, Cathy Cantwell, Perry Schmidt-Leukel and Donald Mitchell. For short single volumes, see John S. Strong, *The Buddha* (2012) and Michael Carrithers, *The Buddha* (2001).

On Jesus, the works are almost too numerous to mention, but the historical Jesus scholarship of figures like John Crossnan, Geza Vermes, Marcus Borg, Ed Sanders is notable. An overview by a conservative Christian is Mark Allan Powell, *Jesus as a Figure in History* (2013). A useful survey is Clinton Bennett, *In Search of Jesus* (2001). For a somewhat different take from an atheist historian, Bart Ehrman's accessible *How Jesus Became God* (2015) is worth reading.

On Muhammad, many introductions to Islam give his life story; David Waines and John Esposito are good authors. For single volume lives, see John Brown, *Muhammad: A Very Short Introduction* (2011), or easy to get hold of is Karen Armstrong's very sympathetic *Muhammad: A Biography of the Prophet* (1993).

On the so-called mythicists, see Maurice Casey, *Jesus: Evidence and Argument or Mythicist Myths?* (2014) and Bart Ehrman, *Did Jesus Exist? The Historical Argument for Jesus of Nazareth* (2013). The mythicists have taken particular offence to Ehrman as a high-profile atheist US scholar with often *ad hominem* attacks.

On debates between Ambedkar and Gandhi, see Ramachandra Guha, 'Gandhi's Ambedkar', at www.ambedkar.org/research/GandhiAmbedkar.htm.

GOD, GODS AND REALITY (CHAPTER 4)

The issues discussed are found in the literature on the philosophy of religion. See articles on topics like 'Philosophy of Religion', 'Theodicy', 'The Problem of Evil' in the Stanford Encyclopaedia of Philosophy (http://plato.stanford.edu) and the Internet Encyclopaedia of Philosophy (www.iep.utm.edu). There are also numerous textbooks and introductions by scholars such as Chad Meister, Linda Zagzebski and Charles Taliaferro. On intersections with atheism, see especially Ruse's works cited in Chapter 1. On the problem of evil, a classic is John Hick, *Evil and the God of Love* (1966).

Elie Wiesel's *Night* (many editions) is worth reading.

On Thich Nhat Hanh, see www.orderofinterbeing.org/about/our-teacher and many other resources online.

Meister Eckhart's Sermons are in various editions. A difficult but good scholarly work is Grace Jantzen, *Power, Gender and Christian Mysticism* (1995).

The translation from Kant's "What is Enlightenment" used here is from Lyman A. Baker, 'Immanuel Kant's "What is Enlightenment":

A Brief Introduction', available at: www.k-state.edu/english/baker/english233/Kant-WIE-intro.htm, accessed 16 September 2015.

On Christian Anti-Semitism, see Ronald Miller, 'Judaism: Siblings in Strife,' in Paul Hedges and Alan Race, eds, *Christian Approaches to Other Faiths* (2008). The classic study is Rosemary Radford Ruether, *Faith and Fratricide: The Theological Roots of Anti-Semitism* (1974).

On Sea of Faith, see their website at www.sofn.org.uk/index.html.

RELIGIONS: THE GOOD, THE BAD AND THE UGLY (CHAPTER 5)

On religion and violence, see Scott Appleby, *The Ambivalence of the Sacred* (2000), Mark Jurgensmeyer, *Terror in the Mind of God* (2003), Perry Schmidt-Leukel, ed., *War and Peace in World Religions* (2004) and Bruce Lincoln, *Holy Terrors* (2003) and Lucien van Liere, 'Terrorism and Violence in the Name of God', in Hedges, *Controversies in Contemporary Religion*, vol. 1.

On non-violence, see Hagen Berndt, *Non-Violence in the World's Religions* (2000) and Ramin Jahanbegloo, *Introduction to Nonviolence* (2014).

On the problematic biblical texts, see Gerd Lüdemann, *The Unholy in Holy Scripture* (1996).

On some of the connections between religion and politics, nationalism and so forth, see Enzo Pace, 'Religion, Nationalism, and International Relations' and Marion Maddox, 'Religion and Politics', both in Hedges, *Controversies in Contemporary Religion*, vol. 2.

On Buddhism, see Jude Lal Fernando, 'Buddhism, Nationalism, and Violence in Asia' in Hedges, *Controversies in Contemporary Religion*, vol. 3.

On Dawkins' meme idea, see dismissals by Ruse (*Atheism*) and McGrath (*Dawkins' God*) and archaeologist Timothy Taylor, 'Artificials, or why Darwin was wrong about humans' and the evolutionary biologist and anthropologist David Sloan Wilson, 'Why Richard Dawkins is wrong about religion', the latter two both in Bentley, *The Edge of Reason?*.

On violence as part of human nature, see useful accessible chapters in Bentley, *The Edge of Reason?*, especially Herbet Maschner and

Katherine Reedy-Maschner, 'The evolution of warfare' and William Calvin, 'Heavens above! Old notions never die. They just incorporate'. On Constantine and Christianity, see Kee, *Constantine versus Christ* (1982).

For the Intelligence Squared Debate on the Catholic Church, see www.intelligencesquared.com/events/the-catholic-church-is-a-force-for-good-in-the-world.

On the Wars of Religion not being about religion, see William Cavanaugh, *The Myth of Religious Violence* (2009) and Wolfgang Palaver, Harriet Rudolph and Dietmar Regensburger, eds, *The European Wars of Religion* (2015).

On radicalization, see Sara Savage, 'Head and Heart in Preventing Religious Radicalization', in Fraser Watts and Geoff Dumbreck, eds, *Head and Heart: Perspectives from Religion and Psychology* (2013). On religion and Islam as not a primary factor, see recent media coverage of research, for example, Anne Aly, 'The Role of Islam in Radicalisation is Grossly Overestimated', *The Guardian* (UK), www.theguardian.com/commentisfree/2015/jan/14/the-role-of-islam-in-radicalisation-is-grossly-overestimated.

On Islamic and Ottoman sources for European and Enlightenment concepts of religious freedom, see discussions at: www.fiqhcouncil. org/node/18 and www.economist.com/blogs/erasmus/2015/02/christianity-islam-and-locke. See also Reza Shah-Kazemi, *The Spirit of Tolerance in Islam* (2012).

On views and dialogue concerning nuclear disarmament in Christianity and Islam, see Shirin Shafaie, 'Bringing Faith Back In': Muslim and Christian Approaches to Nuclear (Non)-Proliferation and Disarmament,' in Paul Hedges, *Contemporary Muslim–Christian Encounters* (2015).

Some may wonder why in the text I have not engaged Stephen Pinker's *Better Angels of Our Nature* (2012), which argues that modernity and its cultural institutions have made us and society better, which he sees as having atheistic implications in that it is not religion which has led to this. While I believe his basic thesis is right that contemporary civil society provides a structure wherein much violence is restrained and that we have in some ways a wider empathy than our ancestors, I find the answer that this is due to some form of humanistic evolution too simplistic. It is clear from examples in New York and elsewhere that changing policing tactics can radically reduce crime, while education and literacy have provided for significant changes in society. Whether this has fundamentally altered human nature and the species propensity for violence and intolerance of others seems, however, a very different issue. Arguing this within the space of this book would not be possible. I am also not sure how far the data actually supports the argument in hand. I include it here, though, as instructive further reading. On the theme of the possible human propensity to war, see Sarah Peacey, 'Have humans always gone to war?', *The Conversation*, https://theconversation.com/have-humans-always-gone-to-war-57321?utm_medium=email&utm_campaign=Latest%20from%20The%20Conversation%20for%20April%2012%202016%20-%20 4656&utm_content=Latest%20from%20The%20Conversation%20 for%20April%2012%202016%20-%204656+CID_.

On women in religion, see Leona Anderson and Pamela Dickey Young, eds, *Women and Religious Traditions* (2015) and Kayla Wheeler, 'Women in Religion: Does Gender Matter?' in Hedges, *Controversies in Contemporary Religion*, vol. 2.

On Islam, see Adis Duderija, 'Sharia Law and Women in Islam,' in Hedges, *Controversies in Contemporary Religion*, vol. 3, and Lynda Clarke's chapter in the Anderson and Young. See also Jerusha Lamptey, 'Unbeknownst to Richard Dawkins the Feminist Revolution in Islam has already Begun,' available at: http://religiondispatches.org/unbeknownst-to-richard-dawkins-the-feminist-revolution-in-islam-has-already-begun.

On homosexuality and gender, see Maria das Dores Campos Machado, 'Sexuality and Religion: Homosexuality and Religious Values' in Hedges, *Controversies in Contemporary Religion*, vol. 2. For Queer Theology, see Elizabeth Stuart, *Gay and Lesbian Theologies* (2003).

For some articles discussing biblical verses on homosexuality, see John Shore, 'The Best Case for the Bible Not Condemning Homosexuality' (2012), at www.huffingtonpost.com/john-shore/the-best-case-for-the-bible-not-condemning-homosexuality_b_1396345.html, and the series of three articles in the *Christian Post* that begin at www.christianpost.com/news/matthew-vines-says-most-christians-are-wrong-homosexuality-is-not-a-sin-82026, and provide arguments on both sides and varied perspectives.

HUMAN ANIMALS, NON-HUMAN ANIMALS AND THE UNIVERSE AROUND US (CHAPTER 7)

On science's relation to religion, see David Lindberg and Ronald Numbers, *God and Nature: Historical Essays on the Encounter Between Christianity and Science* (1986), Edward Grant, *The Foundations of Modern Science in the Middle Ages* (1996), Nancy Morvillo, *Science and Religion: Understanding the Issues* (2010) and Allison P. Coudert, 'Friend or Foe: Current Debates in Science and Religion' in Hedges, *Controversies in Contemporary Religion*, vol. 2. Also useful is Ruse, 'Naturalism and the Scientific Method' in Ruse, *The Oxford Handbook of Atheism*.

On Muslim and Chinese and other involvement in the development of science and related philosophy, see: Dag Nikolaus Hasse, 'Influence of Arabic and Islamic Philosophy on the Latin West', *Stanford Encyclopedia of Philosophy*, available at: http://plato. stanford.edu/entries/arabic-islamic-influence, Toby Huff, *The Rise of Early Modern Science: Islam, China and the West* (1993) and the short video of the 1001 Inventions exhibition showcases some Islamic advances, available at: www.youtube.com/watch?v=JZDe9DCx7Wk. On Tysson's arguments about Islam's failure to develop science, see www.youtube.com/watch?v=fDAT98eEN5Q.

For more on the Galileo issue, see Mario Biagioli, *Galileo, Courtier: The Practise of Science in the Culture of Absolutism* (1993), and on Darwin see McGrath, *Dawkins' God* for an accessible account. For an account of the Wilberforce Huxley debate, see J.R. Lucas, 'Wilberforce and Huxley: A Legendary Encounter' (originally 1979), available at: http://users.ox.ac.uk/~jrlucas/legend.html.

For the facts of evolution, see Jerry Coyne, *Why Evolution is True* (2009). See also, Paula Kover, 'The Five Most Common Misunderstandings about Evolution', http://theconversation.com/ the-five-most-common-misunderstandings-about-evolution-54845.

On the issue of the spheres of 'science' and 'religion' as modern inventions, see Peter Harrison, *The Territories of Science and Religion* (2015).

On Clifford's arguments about bad belief and also William James' counter arguments, see the works cited on the philosophy of religion under Chapter 4.

LIVING IN A RELIGIOUSLY DIVERSE, POST-CHRISTIAN AND POST-SECULAR WORLD (CHAPTER 8)

On secularism, see Jayeel Serrano Cornelio, 'Is Religion Dying? Secularization and Other Religious Trends in the World Today', in Hedges, *Controversies in Contemporary Religion*, vol. 1, and Frank Pasquale and Barry Kosmin, 'Atheism and the Secularization Thesis', in Ruse, *The Oxford Handbook of Atheism*.

On religious diversity and interreligious dialogue, see Paul Hedges, 'Why Are There Many Gods? Religious Diversity and Its Challenges' in Hedges, *Controversies in Contemporary Religion*, vol. 1 and Paul Hedges, *Controversies in Interreligious Dialogue and the Theology of Religions* (2010).

On how religious understanding may help overcome social harm, see Anna Halafoff, 'Riots, Mass Causalities, and Religious Hatred: Countering Anticosmopolitan Terror through Intercultural and Interreligious Understanding' in Hedges, *Controversies in Contemporary Religion*, vol. 2.

On multiple religious belonging, see Rose Drew, 'Christian and Hindu, Jewish and Buddhist: Can You Have a Multiple Religious Identity?' in Hedges, *Controversies in Contemporary Religion*, vol. 1.

On whether religion is more beneficial or harmful in social and psychological ways, and related issues, the anti-religion case is made in Coyne *Faith vs. Fact* and the pro-religion case in McGrath, *Dawkins' God*. For balanced studies, see Ian Reader, 'Public terror versus public good', Andrew Newberg, 'Brain science and belief' and David Sloan Wilson's 'Why Richard Dawkins is wrong about religion', all in Bentley, *The Edge of Reason?* and Phil Zuckerman, 'Atheism and Societal Health', in Ruse, *The Oxford Handbook of Atheism*. A classic survey of studies is Harold G. Koenig and Harvey J. Cohen, *The Link Between Religion and Health: Psychoneuroimmunology and the Faith Factor* (2001). For some research about the roots of altruism, see Jo Cutler, 'Are you a true altruist or driven by self-interest? Brain scan may give verdict', *The Conversation*, https://theconversation.com/are-you-a-true-altruist-or-driven-by-self-interest-brain-scan-may-give-verdict-55545.

On studies on the relation between wealth and compassion, see the report in *Scientific American*, Daisy Grewal, 'How Wealth Reduces Compassion', www.scientificamerican.com/article/how-wealth-reduces-compassion, and Paul Piff's TED talk on his research, 'Does Money Make you Mean,' www.ted.com/talks/paul_piff_does_money_make_you_mean?language=en.

On the Masters of Suspicion, see Rick Roderick's lecture, available at: www.youtube.com/watch?v=4wetwETy4u0.

INDEX

0 (number), 142

A Thousand and One Nights, 52
Abraham, 57, 66
Abrahamic religions, 25, 74, 87, 169
    God of, 49
age of consent, 69–70
agnosticism (agnostic), 9, 33, 54,
    74, 77, 85, 88, 89, 168
Aisha, 68–70, 125
al-Ghazali, Muhammad, 83, 141–2
Allah, 100, 125
    as (most) merciful, 38, 101
    meaning God, 49
    see also God
Ambedkar, Bhimrao, 72
Anaximander, 24
anti-Semitism, 86, 185
    see Judaism
Appleby, Scott, 'ambivalence
    of the sacred', 101
archaeology, 46, 47, 144
Arendt, Hannah, 105
Aristotle (Aristotelianism), 138–9,
    149, 150, 151, 154, 156, 177
as-Asadi, Taqi al-Din, 15
atheism (atheists)
    amongst scientists, 16, 139
    ancient Greek legacy, 24, 131
    atheist churches, 89, 169, 171–2
    causes of/foundations for
        (hard sciences, humanities,
        philosophy, social sciences),
        15–16, 50, 144, 154–5

Confucian, 24, 25, 161–2
    defined against belief in God, 23–4
    definition of, 22–26, 76, 77
    fundamentalist, 50, 117
    moral arguments for (as moral
        choice), 25–6, 90–1, 161–2, 163
    New Atheism, 10, 96, 156, 181
    relation to religion, 14–18,
        88–90, 94–5, 112, 179
    stereotyped and/ or persecuted
        18–19, 91, 161
Augustine of Hippo, 103, 177

Bacon, Francis, 143
Bait al-Hikmah ('House of
    Wisdom'), 142
Barbour, Ian, 156
Beatitudes, 163
Beauvoir, Simone de, 163, 171
Beguinages, 132
belief/faith, atheism and belief, 26, 77
    better founded (more
        credible), 34, 55
    definition/usage, 26–9
    does science need faith?, 34–5
    doubt as part of, 89–90
    faith versus reason, 18, 26-35
    faith versus science, 157–8
    leap of faith, 34
    religious faith similar to other
        forms of belief, 30, 32–3
    terms used interchangeably, 28
    see also rationality
Bellarmine, Cardinal, 152

Benedict of Nursia, 47
Bible, 1 Corinthians, 113, 121–2
    1 Timothy, 113
    2 Maccabees, 44
    Acts of Peter, 45
    Acts of the Apostles, 48, 61, 64–5
    Book of Job, 83
    canon, 36, 42–8
    collection of New Testament
        Canon, 44–7, 48, 53
    Genesis, 92, 113, 130,
        131, 146, 147
    Gnostic Bible, 44
    Gospel of John, 65, 102
    Gospel of Luke, 102, 120
    Gospel of Mark, 61
    Gospel of Matthew, 102
    Gospel of Thomas, 45
    Latin, 39, 65
    Leviticus, 113
    Lost Gospels, 46
    Old Testament/Hebrew Bible,
        42–4, 76, 92, 98, 144
    New Testament, 37, 40, 113
    Philemon, Letter to, 123
    Philippians, Letter to, 123
    reliability of New Testament, 46–7
    Romans, Letter to, 122
    scripture made by community/
        tradition, 40, 44, 47, 48, 49
    Septuagint, 43
    Song of Songs, 146
    Ten Commandments, 163
    texts of terror, 98
    see also interpretation, Jesus,
        specific names
Borg, Marcus, 61
Botton, Alain de, 89, 171–2
Brahe, Tycho, 15, 150, 151
Bruno, Giordano, 150
Buddha (Buddhism), 51, 57;
    60, 71, 88, 95, 104, 115,
    131, 165, 169, 171, 175
    as non-theism, 76–7
    as optimistic, 87

    atheist use of (as atheist), 9–10,
        25, 89, 97, 161, 179
    Buddha as human or deity, 65
    Buddha compared to/contrasted
        with Jesus, 61, 64
    Dhammapada, 51
    life and teachings of Buddha, 62–3,
        67–8, 72, 72–3, 87, 174
    gods in, 20, 21, 76–7, 87, 132
    Guanyin, 132
    Mahayana, 174
    nuns, 124
    peace and violence in, 107–8
    samsara (world of rebirth and
        impermanence), 77, 87, 174
    Theravada (Sri Lankan),
        108, 174, 176, 179
    wisdom and compassion, 95
    Zen, 94
    see also compassion, meditation,
        Nagarjuna, Thich Nhat Hanh
Butler, Judith, 130

Calvin, John, 148, 151
Capra, Fritjof, The Tao of Physics, 156–7
China (Chinese), 98, 111,
    142, 161, 164, 169
    cultural revolution, 166
    gender norms and roles, 123–4, 132
    human and divine in, 67, 73
    landscape painting, 17
    levels of religions experience in, 166
    role in development of science,
        140–1, 154, 188
    Three Great Inventions, 140–1
Christianity, as originally Jewish, 44
    creeds, 47–8, 55
    creation ex nihilo, 92
    Death of God theologians, 88
    evangelical (fundamentalist), 22,
        40, 41, 42, 51, 53, 55, 58, 80,
        91, 110, 111, 112–13, 146,
        147, 148, 153, 156, 162
    Gnosticism, 45–6, 64
    Liberation Theology, 162
    Nestorian Church, 101

peace and violence in, 101–104, 105
Pentecostalism, 80, 162
Process Theology, 88
Prosperity Gospel, 162
Reformation, 38-9, 40,
    43–4, 65, 104
Queer Theology, 131, 134
role of women (patriarchy),
    118, 119–23, 129, 131
see also Bible, Jesus, Roman
    Catholicism, specific names
Cicero, 52
Clifford, William Kingdom, 158, 188
colonialism (imperialism), 103,
    104, 106, 127, 128, 179
Comfort, Roy, 80
compassion , 37, 38, 84, 87, 95,
    130, 132, 163, 172, 173–6;
    karuna/metta, 174, 175, 176
Comte, Auguste, 89
confirmation bias, 167
Confucius (Confucianism),
    21, 57, 70, 169, 172
Analects, 18
atheist use of, 17–18, 24, 25, 161–2
human nature 176
tian ('sky/heaven'), 18; 169
see also ritual, Mencius, Xunzi
Constantine (emperor), 103, 114
Coperncius, Nicholas, 149–50, 151
Coyne, Jerry, 16, 97, 148,
    154, 157–9, 167, 181
Creationism, 117, 145–6, 147, 156
see also evolution

Daly, Mary, 119, 134
Daoism, 57, 94, 140, 166
Celestial Masters Lineage, 169
Daodejing, 57, 83, 123
Laozi, 57, 123
Quanzhen Dao, 123–4
role of women, 123–4, 133
yin-yang, 123
Zhuangzi, 27, 35
Darwin, Charles, 31, 50, 144–5,
    155, 157, 171, 179
loss of faith, 50, 144

On The Origin of Species, 50, 144, 145
Dawkins, Richard, 10, 22, 34, 50,
    80, 96, 97, 116–7, 159, 171
deism (deist), 17, 75, 86, 154
democracy, 106, 125, 127, 172
Democritus, 24
Dennett, Daniel, 96, 114, 164–5
Derrida, Jacques, 54
Descartes, René, 27, 28, 35
Durkheim, Émile, 81, 171

Eagleton, Terry, 10
Eckhart (Meister), 76, 83, 94, 95
Einstein, Albert, 15
Engels, Friedrich, 49, 119
Enlightenment (European), 10, 24,
    25, 39, 53, 75, 78–9, 114-5, 129,
    131, 147, 148, 161–2, 177, 179
'What is Enlightenment?', 78–9
eschatology (apocalyptic, end of the
    world), 39, 60, 72, 101–102, 165
Evans, Dylan, 167, 182
evil, problem of, (theodicy), 75,
    78, 83–8, 90–1, 92-3
evolution (theory of), 50, 117,
    137, 144–8, 155, 158
see also Oxford debate,
    Darwin, Charles

faith *see* belief
feminism (feminist), 127, 130, 134
Buddhist, 72
Enlightenment, 129
gender construction,
    129–30, 131, 134
Hindu, 128
Islamic, 126, 127
early Christianity as proto-
    feminist, 120, 123
goddess spirituality, 134
matriarchal society, 119, 130
naturalist, 130
sexism, 13, 119, 133–4, 135
theology, 88, 119–20, 121–2
see also goddess, patriarchy,
    science, 'role of women'
    in specific religions
freethinker, 24, 25, 26, 40

Freud, Sigmund, 162, 163–4
Fry, Stephen, 108

Gadamer, Hans-Georg, 167
Galileo Galilei, 147, 148–53, 156
    trial, 151–2
    *Dialogue Concerning the Two
      Chief World Systems*, 152
Gandhi, Mohandas (Mahatma),
    37, 38, 51, 53, 72
Global Ethic, 175
God, arguments for, 78–83
    and language, 82–3, 89, 93
    see also Allah, evil, problem
      of, goddess
goddess, 74, 77, 119, 128,
    132, 133, 134, 135
Gould, Stephen Jay, 156
Gregory of Nazianzus, 83

Harris, Sam, 22, 89, 96, 159, 181
    on Buddhism, 9–10, 97
Heliocentric universe, 149, 150, 158
Hell (eternal), 83, 103, 113, 144
Heresy, 61, 93, 103, 152
Heyward, Carter, 88, 89
Hick, John, 84
Hilda of Whitby, 132
Hinduism, 22, 57–8, 74–5,
    76, 87, 94, 104, 115
    Advaita, 75, 94
    atheism in, 22, 23
    Bhagavad Gita, 37, 53, 57
    Dalits, 72
    dharma, 37
    karma, 87
    Laws of Manu, 128
    peace and violence in, 107–108
    Ramayana, 51
    role of women in, 128–9
    Shiva Nataraja, 17
    suttee (self-immolation of
      wives), 128–9
    Swaminaryan, 58
    Upanishads, 76
    Vedas, 75, 76
    Vishnu/Krishna, 37, 57, 74
    see also Gandhi, yoga

Hitchens, Christopher, 22, 26,
    58, 73, 96, 108, 179, 181
Homer, 22, 52
homosexuality, 112–13
    in Bible, 113
    homophobia, 112
human flourishing, 53, 54
human rights, 98, 110–13,
    114–17, 118, 172
    freedom of religion and
      belief, 114, 116–17
    right to teach children
      religion, 116–7, 164-5
    slavery, 53, 110–11, 113, 146–7
    Universal Declaration of
      Human Rights, 114
Humanism (humanist), 9, 25, 26,
    53, 89, 171, 174, 179, 186
Hume, David, 81
Huxley, Thomas, 144–5

Ibn Sina, 149, 156
identity construction, 19, 30, 33,
    90, 91, 108, 112, 128, 134,
    135, 168, 170, 171, 172
    in-group and out-group, 178
    multiple religious identity, 169
Ignatius of Loyola, 47
imaginary associations, friends, 165
intellectual humility, 33
inter-being, 94–5
    see also Thich Nhat Hanh
interreligious dialogue, 164, 178–9
Internet revolution, 140
interpretation (hermeneutics) (of
    scripture), 36–42, 47–50,
    52, 53, 102, 145, 156
    accommodationism, 148, 151
    allegory, 82–3, 87
    of law and constitution, 49
    authorial intention, 38
    competing schools of, 38, 53
    context, 99
    historical-critical approach, 39, 40
    historical development, 38
    interpreting community (societies,
      creatures), 37, 38, 47, 49

literal reading (as act of
    interpretation, as modern),
    38, 39, 40–2, 53, 146
Origen's hermeneutics, 29, 38
proof-texting, 99
text as interpretation of
    the community, 40
theological more sophisticated than
    fundamentalist or atheist, 40
    see also Bible, Qur'an
Irenaeus of Lyon, 84
Islam (Muslim), 16, 25, 49, 57,
    66–7, 87, 92, 97, 103, 105, 106,
    145, 148, 149, 169, 170, 174
    and science, 15, 29, 141–2, 149, 154
    Australian Aboriginal Muslims, 169
    bila kayf ('without asking why?'), 141
    divorce, 125, 126
    fatwa, 116
    female leadership in Islam, 125
    freedom of religion in, 115–16
    Islamic law (Shariah), 69,
        116, 124, 126, 127
    Islamophobia, 22
    itjihad, 116
    jihad, 101
    peace and violence in, 36–7, 38,
        70–1, 99–101, 105–106, 107
    Pact of Umar, 115
    People of the Book, 115
    role of women in, 124–8
    Sufism, 76, 93, 94
    veiling/hijab,126–7
    Wahhabism, 107
    see also Muhammad, Qur'an,
        specific names

Jantzen, Grace, 95
Japan, religious belief in, 166, 169
Jedi, 170
Jerome, 147
Jesus, 39, 43, 44, 45, 46, 47, 48,
    63, 64, 70, 71, 80, 91, 103,
    122, 131, 132, 146, 170, 176
    as apocalyptic prophet, 72, 102
    as ethical teacher, 67
    attitude towards women, 120, 123

historical figure, 58–9, 67, 73
    human or divine, 37, 40, 61, 64–7
    life and teachings, 52, 59–61, 162
    pacifism and violence,101–102, 104
John of the Cross, 94
Judaism, 21, 22; 42–3, 57, 66, 87,
    92, 129–30, 135, 169, 170
    atheist, 88
    Holocaust, 86, 87, 88, 105
    peace and violence in, 99
    Rabbinic Judaism, 43
    supersessionism (Christian
        attitude), 43
    see also Bible, specific names

Kant, Immanuel, 78–80, 82
    'What is Enlightenment?', 78–9
Kepler, Johannes, 150, 151
    Epitome Astromoniae
        Copernicae, 150
Khadija, 68–9, 125
Kierkegaard, Søren, 34
King, Martin Luther, 51–2
Küng, Hans, 175
Kurtz, Paul, 15

Lamarck, Jean-Baptiste, 155
Lamptey, Jerusha, 127
law of double effect, 54
Leonardo da Vinci, 17
Li Bai, 52
liberal (progressive) (religion, theology,
    Christianity), 65, 72, 81, 134,
    146, 147, 148, 177, 178
Lisbon earthquake (1755), 85
literacy, 143, 144, 154
Locke, John, 115
Luther, Martin, 43, 47
Lyell, Charles, 144, 145

Marcion, 44
Marx, Karl (Marxism, Communism),
    30, 32, 33, 49, 71, 98, 104
    Christian dialogue with, 164
    critique of religion, 162, 163
    similarity to religion, 20, 49
    see also Engels, Friedrich

Masters of Suspicion, 162–4
meaning (in life), 51, 73, 88,
    95, 169, 170–1, 178
    humans as meaning creating
    creatures, 55, 166
meditation, 62, 68, 82, 87,
    94, 159, 169, 170
    mindfulness, 62, 94, 95
Mencius, 91, 173, 176
    Ox Mountain, 176
    see also Confucius
Middle Ages (medieval), 29, 39,
    54, 65, 68, 70, 95, 103, 105,
    116, 129, 131, 132, 138–9,
    142, 154, 155, 157, 176, 177
miracles (miraculous), 32, 39,
    58, 59, 63, 64, 81, 87,
Moghul Dynasty, 142
Mongol, sack of Baghdad, 142
Monotheism, 66–7, 74–5, 76, 88, 169;
    and problem of evil, 78, 87, 88
Morality (ethics), and problem
    of evil, 84–5
    jihad as moral struggle, 101
    moral grounding of beliefs, 158
    moral revolt against religion,
        24–5, 90–1, 144
    possible without God (within
        atheism), 18–19, 25–6, 53, 161
    potential atheist-religious dialogue
        on, 26, 53–4, 160–4, 173–6
    religion as morally deficient,
        51, 110, 164
    religion concerned with moral
        truths/sphere, 148, 156
    science and morality, 159
    see also compassion, human flourishing
Moses, 57, 66
Mother Teresa, 109
Muhammad, 66, 99, 125, 126, 127
    as 'a mercy to the world', 68
    criticisms of, 68–71, 72
    sayings of (hadith), 49, 101
    see also Aisha, Khadijah

multicultural (multireligious,
    diverse) societies, 142, 172
    coexistence, 171, 172
mysticism, 76, 81, 94, 95, 142, 154
    see also spirituality, specific names

Nagarjuna, 83
Nanak (Guru), 51, 70
Napoleon, Bonaparte, 155
nationalism, 20, 30, 32, 33, 34, 98,
    103, 104, 105, 107–108, 128, 158
natural law, 26, 173
naturalistic world view, 23, 81
Newberg, Andrew, 167
Newton, Isaac, 15, 143, 154, 155
Nietzsche, Friedrich, 162–3, 171
NOMA (non-overlapping
    magisteria), 156
'nones' (religious), 179
non-violence (ahimsa, pacifism), 37,
    38, 53, 72, 102, 103, 104, 175
    see specific religions, specific names

Ockham's Razor (William of Ockham),
    15, 139, 140, 157, 159
Origen, 38, 39, 41, 147
Ottoman empire, 115, 142
Oxford debate (1860, on
    evolution), 144–5
    see also Huxley, Thomas,
        Wilberforce, Samuel

Paganism, 20, 75, 77, 94, 100,
    133, 135, 169, 170, 171
Paine, Thomas, 17
Paley, William, 177
panentheism, 76, 86, 88
pantheism, 20, 75, 86, 88
Parliament of the World's
    Religions (1893), 178
    World Parliament of Religions
        (1993), 175
patriarchy, 39, 40, 57, 130–4, 135, 136
    see also feminism, 'role of women'
        in specific religions

Paul (Apostle/St), 44, 45, 47, 65, 102
    on women, 120–3, 130
Philosophy, 9, 10, 17, 20, 23, 25, 27,
    34, 50, 51, 54, 64, 71, 75, 76, 77,
    78–80, 81, 82–8, 89, 92, 94, 115,
    131, 138, 139, 140, 141, 149,
    157–8, 161, 163, 165, 167, 177
    Buddhist, 25, 83
    Confucian, 21, 24, 25, 173
    Daoist, 27, 83
    empiricism, 138
    etymological fallacy, 23
    Hindu, 21, 23, 75, 76, 82
    idealism, 138
    Islamic, 83
    Jewish, 75
    logical fallacies, 167
    study of related to atheism, 16
    see also Ockham's Razor,
        specific names
Pinker, Stephen, Better Angels
    of Our Nature, 187–8
Plato, (Platonism, Neo-Platonism),
    51, 129, 131, 138, 177
Pliny the Elder, 89, 154
Pol Pot, 105
polytheism, 21, 75, 76, 100
pope, see Roman Catholicism
prayer, 24, 44, 77, 82, 86,
    90, 93, 100, 143
Prisca and Aquila, 122
psychology, 30, 71, 92, 163–4
Ptolemaeus, Claudius (Ptolemy)
    (ptolemaic cosmology),
    149, 150, 152
    Almagest, 149

Quakers, 40, 104
Queen Elizabeth I, 71
Queen of Sheba, 125
Qur'an, 38, 49, 51, 98–101,
    110, 125, 126, 127, 147
    sword verse, 100–101

rationality (reason), as aspect
    of faith/belief, 28, 34

contrasted with faith/belief/religion,
    14–15, 18, 26–34, 139, 157–8
rational, irrational, arational
    (distinction), 26, 34
rational religion, 75
related to atheism, 25–6
relation to gender construction,
    129–30, 131
religious opposing secular
    instrumental, 111
roots in ancient Greece, 138
suspension (bracketing out) of, 31, 34
see also belief/faith, philosophy
Reimarus, Hermann Samuel, 40
reincarnation, 154, 174
religion, definition, 19–22, 182
    essentialism in definitions,
        104, 110, 177
    natural/normal (evolutionary
        explanations for), 32,
        157, 165–6, 168
    death throes, 164
    is religion harmful?, 96–8
    problems of defining, 20
    religious people (contrasted with
        non-religious, and problem of
        the terminology when used
        pejoratively), 14–5, 17, 18–19,
        21, 22, 26, 28, 32, 33, 89–90,
        97, 157, 165, 167, 171
    types of theism (monotheism,
        pantheism, polytheism,
        panentheism, ietism, henotheism,
        deism, nontheisms), 74–8
    see also atheism, specific religions
religious (spiritual) experience,
    80–2, 166–67
    dopamine, 167
    measured across cultures, 166
Renaissance, 25, 43, 138,
    141, 142, 154
    twelfth century, 138
rituals (ceremonial), 82, 113, 164,
    165, 169, 170, 171–2
    and Confucianism, 24,
        162, 172, 176

Roman Catholicism, 43–4, 103,
    118, 148–9, 151–3
  Benedict XVI, 109
  Council of Trent, 148
  Francis I, 109–10, 153
  Index of Prohibited Books, 152
  John Paul II, 152, 153
  Office of the Inquisition, 98, 152
  Paul III, 149
  Purgatory, 103
  source of good/evil in
      world, 108–10
  Urban VIII, 151, 152
  see also Christianity, specific names
Ruether, Rosemary Radford, 119–20
Rumi, 22, 51, 83
Ruse, Michael, 26, 59

Sappho, 52
Sartre, Jean-Paul, 50, 163, 171
Schweitzer, Albert, 102
science, ancient Greek roots, 138–9
  Baconian model, 142–3
  does science need faith?, 34–5
  hypothesis (meaning), 34–5
  induction and deduction
      (method) 143
  myth of war between religion
      and science, 137–8, 154–5
  role of religion in development,
      15, 139–43
  science as anti-religious and
      relationship to religion, 155–9
  sexism in, 118, 133, 136; study of
      not leading to atheism, 15–16
  see also evolution, Ockham's
      Razor, specific names
Sea of Faith, 88
secularism (secular, secularisation),
    18–19; 52, 54, 88, 98, 104–5,
    111–12, 114–15, 116, 125,
    127, 128–9, 131, 132, 134,
    135, 154, 164, 175, 177
sexual intercourse, in Judaism,
    129–30, 135
  in Paganism, 135
  in Zoroastrianism, 135

Shakespeare, 22, 28, 51, 52, 78
Shinto, 169
Singapore, 49, 73
Socrates, 24
spiritual but not religious, 94, 170
spirituality (spiritual), 9, 39, 47, 51, 52,
    70, 71, 75, 76, 82, 86, 88, 89, 93–
    5, 143, 154, 155, 168, 169, 170–2
  defined, 93
  in atheism, 19, 170–1
  in Confucianism, 18, 21
  in Daoism, 123–4, 133
  in Islam, 101
  related to gender, 123–4,
      133, 134, 175
  relation to mysticism, 94
  see also mysticism
Star Wars, 170
Stuart, Elizabeth, 134
Sunzi, Art of War, 51

terrorism, 105–106, 107, 116
  9/11, 179
  Al-Qaeda, 106, 107
  and Western foreign policy, 106
  ISIS/Daesh, 105, 106
  Taliban, 106
  radicalization, 106, 107
Thales, 24
The Matrix, 28
The Missionary, 111
Thich Nhat Hanh, 94–5
Thomas Aquinas (Thomism), 26,
    40–1, 54, 79, 82, 105, 147,
    149, 151, 154, 156, 177
Tillich, Paul, Theology of
    Correlation, 52, 177
Turkey, 125, 127, 166
Tyson, Neil deGrasse, 109, 141

Übermensch, 163

via negativa (way of negation), 82–3
violence (warfare), just war, 105, 175
  religious, 12, 19, 36–7, 53,
      70, 86, 98–108
  see also non-violence, Wars of
      Religion, specific religions

Vanini, Giulio Cesare, 24
Voltaire, 85, 179

Wars of Religion (European), 98, 115
Weinberg, Stephen, 105
Whitmarsh, Tim, 89
Wiesel, Elie, 86
Wilberforce, Samuel, 144–5
Williams, Rowan, 89

women *see* feminism, goddess,
    patriarchy, 'role of women' in
    specific religions, specific names
Xunzi, 21, 24, 162, 174, 176, 179
    see also Confucius, ritual

yoga, 37, 94, 169, 170

Young, William P., *The Shack*, 91

Paul Hedges is Associate Professor of Interreligious Studies at RSIS, Nanyang Technological University, Singapore, and has previously worked for British, Canadian, and Chinese universities. He is the author and editor of several books around his research interests in the meeting and debate between worldviews. Find out more about Dr Hedges at his website www.logosdao.wordpress.com